ALIENS OVER KENTUCKY

THE FRIGHTENING FLOYDS

Anubis Press
Louisville, KY

Thank you for reading! If you like the book, please leave a review on Amazon and Goodreads. Even if you don't like it, please still leave a review.

To keep up with more Anubis Press news, join the Anubis Press Dynasty on Facebook

Also by The Frightening Floyds

Louisville's Strange and Unusual Haunts
Kentucky's Haunted Mansions
Haunts of Hollywood Stars and Starlets
Indiana's Strange and Unusual Haunts
Be Our Ghost

ALIENS OVER KENTUCKY

THE FRIGHTENING FLOYDS

ANUBIS PRESS

This book is dedicated to Jacob's father, David Floyd. It was his love of science fiction that sparked his son's interest in the extraterrestrial.

ALIENS OVER KENTUCKY

THE FRIGHTENING FLOYDS

TABLE OF CONTENTS

Onto Aliens: An Introduction to Another World

About the Authors

Bibliography

Photo Credits

Also Available from Anubis Press

ONTO ALIENS: AN INTRODUCTION TO ANOTHER WORLD

For a couple of years now we have brought to you tales of ghosts and other paranormal legends. We have decided to take a break from the spiritual realm for a bit and are now welcoming you into the world of the extraterrestrial. It's not just specters and phantoms we are interested in, we also have a fascination with UFOs and aliens. While Kentucky is clearly one of the most haunted states in the nation, there are more than just ghost stories there; it also has quite a history of extraterrestrial encounters.

Kentucky has UFO sightings, crop circles, cattle mutilations, encounters with strange, humanoid creatures, mysterious lights in the sky, and even an abduction case. We've even had a UFO chase, police battling with an unknown craft, and a meat shower. Some of Kentucky's most famous alien stories are included in this collection: the Stanford abductions, the Thomas Mantell crash, the train and UFO collision, the dogfight over General Electric, the Kelly Creatures, and many more. So whether you're interested in tracking triangles or saucers through the sky, unexplained radar interruptions, leaping freaks that breathe fire, or a boxing legend's claims that he has seen UFOs, we got a little bit of everything for you in *Aliens over Kentucky*.

Of course, we understand that some of these accounts could be fictitious. We never like to say something is a hoax and walk away. We like to give people the benefit of the doubt. What some people claim is a hoax may simply be a misinterpretation of the events reported. Much as we do with ghost stories, we like to take people on good faith instead of with a grain of salt. We feel that makes for a more open-ended investigation, which is good because these cases are far from closed.

Also, some stories could have human explanations, such as Spring-heeled Jack or the UFO-train collision. There have been perfectly "reasonable" explanations regarding those reports, explanations that are more scientific or "realistic". However, we also realize that even if those explanations sound convincing, they may be incorrect. Much the same as one requires irrefutable evidence to prove aliens exist, one also needs solid evidence to debunk any claims. So while someone may be able to say, "That UFO is a weather balloon," unless there is undeniable evidence to prove that the weather balloon was the object reported, it's still open for discussion.

There are certainly factors to consider when analyzing Kentucky UFO claims. If aliens did exist, and they were interested in settling on Earth in relative secrecy, Kentucky would be ideal. Not only are there numerous hills, mountains, and wooded areas where they could hide, there are also the vast labyrinths of Mammoth Cave. An alien race could possibly build an entire civilization in that massive subterranean warren. If they were here and our government wanted to monitor (or conceal) them, they would probably set up or use installations nearby, such as the Bluegrass Army Depot, Fort Campbell, and Fort Knox, all of which have had alleged connections to UFO activity, according to UFOlogists and eyewitness reports.

What else makes Kentucky ideal? It lies just outside of an area known for high UFO traffic. That location is the Great Serpent Mound in Ohio, which is not far from the bulk of Kentucky's alien activity. We will go into more detail about that (and all the other reports) in the book.

So when you ponder all reports of alien activity in the state, it's hard to believe that there is nothing strange going on. Perhaps not every account truly involves extraterrestrials, but there are a few stories here that can make a believer out of an open-minded individual. Even if you're a hardcore skeptic, the stories are still intriguing, even if you're goal is simply to debunk them. While there are many attempted explanations for UFO sightings and alien encounters that don't really add up and are not too convincing, others seem more viable. Every explanation and debunking only helps us find answers sooner, as it could possibly eliminate that which is not alien from the equation. That is why an open-mind to the point of cognitive dissonance is important when researching UFO and alien sightings.

However, even with all the theories and accounts out there, this book is meant solely for entertainment. It is not an attempt to validate or discredit any stories or claims written about herein. While we have seen some unidentified craft and had some unexplainable situations ourselves, we realize that they might have explanations that do not involve aliens.

Furthermore, while we certainly believe in the possibility and the probability that life exists elsewhere in the universe, we also understand that no cold hard proof yet exists, or has been made public, and that no reports in this book are conclusive. We also understand that while life may exist on other planets, that doesn't necessarily mean they can, have, or will visit Earth. Many cases can be attributed to very mundane celestial events, secret government and military training and technology, and others can simply be hoaxes. While we do not like to claim anything is a hoax, we certainly understand that the possibility is very real.

At the same time, we keep our minds open to both ends of the spectrum. It is very possible that aliens have visited Earth, continue to visit, and are still here. While it has not been proven they exist, it has also not been proven that they don't, and most of these cases have not been conclusively debunked. In fact, many have been attributed to explanations that simply don't make sense. It is our belief that to be able to report such cases correctly, one has to keep a completely open mind to not only the idea that all cases may be mundane, but all cases might truly be aliens. There is a lot in the universe we do not understand, so for anyone to say they have all the answers is impossible.

We compiled the information ahead through extensive online research, and all sources are listed in the bibliography section at the end of the book. We combed methodically through the sources, cross-referenced them with other sources, and checked numerous sites and search engines to see what we could uncover. We always attempt to be as accurate as possible, so any misinformation is unintentional. This book is not meant to be a reference guide or any sort of scientific or historic manual. Again, it is strictly for entertainment purposes, intended for those who are fans of extraterrestrial reports.

We hope you enjoy the book. Please leave us a review, whether you liked it or not. Reviews help authors, and they are very much appreciated.

Thank you for reading *Aliens Over Kentucky,*

The Frightening Floyds

DOGFIGHT OVER GENERAL ELECTRIC

It sounds like something out of a science fiction novel, or something that would happen on a late night, black & white, B-movie, but it isn't. It was real and it happened in Louisville, Kentucky over the General Electric Appliance Park on February 26th, 1993.

Two air patrolmen—Kenny Downs and Kenny Graham—began the night in routine fashion. They arrived at work around 6pm and went about their regular patrols for most of the evening. Around midnight, they received a call about a break-in near Sanford Avenue and Buechel Bank Road, close to where the GE compound is located. As they were spotlighting the area, Graham, an eleven-year veteran, thought he saw one of the many bonfires that were common around the area during the winter months. He called his partner's attention to it and Downs, a five-year veteran at the time, turned the 1.3 million-candle-power spotlight on and shined it at the lights. That's when they both saw a strange spherical object glowing in the sky. When the spotlight hit it, the object began to drift back into the darkness, and then began moving back and forth before floating up level with the helicopter while hovering in the air.

Graham later said that the strange ball began to move at an unusually high speed, circling counterclockwise until it reached the rear of the chopper. Graham sped up to 100mph to try to out-maneuver the persistent orb, but it shot right past them and began flying circles around the

1

helicopter. Next, the object rose into the air and descended on the chopper before taking off.

Perplexed but determined to discover what they were dealing with, Graham tried to catch the mysterious craft. As he approached it, fireballs suddenly began to shoot from its center, causing the pilot to retreat. When he doubled back to catch the shooter, it had vanished from sight.

After landing and returning to base, Graham decided to call the control tower at Louisville International Airport to inquire if someone had spotted anything peculiar on radar. No one had. Downs phoned dispatch and asked if they had any calls that night regarding strange lights in the sky but found his search just as fruitless.

Two ground patrol officers, Mike Smith and Joe Smolenski, confirmed the sighting. Smith saw the object fire before it disappeared; Smolenski tried to chase it down, but the object was too fast. He stated that he had been looking for aliens for fourteen years and wasn't about to pass up this opportunity. He later said this would probably be the closest he ever got to them.

Lt. David Pope described both Graham and Downs as solid guys. He vouched for their word by stating that if they said something was out there, he had no doubt something out there.

At the time, one of Jenny's family members was a long-time employee of General Electric. She recalls him coming home that night stating that he had seen the helicopters chasing something over GE. Rumor around the plant was that the helicopters were in pursuit of a UFO. She thought he was either lying or just putting her on because he knew how much she loved *E.T.* But, she would later find out that his story was true.

This was not the only tie General Electric ever had with alleged alien encounters. It seems that their history with the extraterrestrial goes back nearly forty-years prior to this occasion.

Some UFO archival sites have recorded a history of GE's involvement with supposed government experiments as far back as the 1950s. Along with the Glenn L. Martin Co., Bell Aircraft, Sperry-Rand, and numerous other large companies, General Electric had been working with the Department of Defense on anti-gravity projects. It was said they had built the anti-gravity engines for the disks the United States had created, prompting some to believe they would have had to use alien technology to develop such devices.

The Department of Defense became official on September 18th, 1947. President Truman signed it into being via the National Security Act of 1947, known as the National Military Establishment. This act also created the National Security Resources Board, the National Security Council, the Army Air Force (later to become the United States Air Force), the Joint Chiefs of Staff, and the Central Intelligence Agency. This evolved from Truman's proposal to create the act at the end of World War II in an effort to beef up national security.

Only two months before that, on July 7th, Walter Haut, public information officer of the Roswell Army Air Field, issued a press release stating that they had recovered a flying disk that crashed somewhere near the base. Rumors and speculations about alien life held at Roswell began, and caused a sensation among those who believe in aliens that is still at the center of UFO debates. This might make some wonder if Truman was trying to protect the nation from international threats, or from interstellar.

Numerous UFO sky-watcher sites around the Internet claim that on June 5th, 1965, UFOs were spotted over a GE plant in Lynn, Massachusetts, but no details are registered. However, just ten days later, on June 15th, 1965, there is a report from the National Investigations Committee on Aerial Phenomenon about a possible UFO spotted in an apartment complex in Lynn.

William Angelos had been at home on Henry Street watching television when he heard a rhythmic thumping, like pistons in a car engine, rumbling outside his apartment. When he stepped out onto his porch, which was located on the ground floor, he saw a red light in the air over the parking lot about twenty-feet beyond the courtyard. The glow appeared to be emanating from the base of a flat, colorless, disk-shaped craft with a domed top. The ship was hovering about twelve feet above the ground next to the wall of a nearby building. After a few minutes, the disk ascended slowly into the air and vanished to the west-southwest.

Though no one else in the apartment complex reported seeing this shining saucer, others in the vicinity did confess to hearing the thumps and seeing odd lights outside their windows. Others reported having issues with the reception on their televisions.

A more infamous incident occurred in Schenectady, NY above the original General Electric plant in December of 1973, witnessed by many but reported by two women who were on their way to the Mohawk Mall to do some Christmas shopping. The two women, named Carol and Louise, saw a strange craft coming in slowly from the west. When it reached the GE plant, the ship hovered over top of it for a second. Suddenly, all the lights in the facility slowly dimmed and faded out. They thought, at first, that it might have been a citywide blackout, but soon saw that all other lights in the city were blazing.

On the highway, about a hundred yards from the plant, traffic came to a halt as spectators emerged from their vehicles to gawk at the unbelievable spectacle they had just witnessed. Louise described the craft as a saucer-shaped object about the size of two or three football fields in diameter, with rotating blue, pink, and yellow lights at the base; the top, she said, was a dull gray.

For about five to ten minutes, the saucer hovered silently as all lights on its underside dimmed into a soft yellow glow. Then, it rose into the air and travelled back into the west. Carol and Louise returned to their cars and drove on, listening to the radio for any reports. Several people called in to report the happening, and there was press coverage on it over the next couple of days. In the end, the military said it was just Air Force maneuvers.

In 1973, GE released a small transistor radio called the UFO or Flying Saucer P2775A Radio, and it had a flat base and a domed top. The device was manufactured in the Bridgeport, CT and Syracuse, NY facilities. Bridgeport, CT is about 163 miles west-southwest of Lynn, Massachusetts while Syracuse is 127 miles west of Schenectady, NY. This means both the UFO in Lynn spotted by William Angelos and the UFO in Schenectady spotted by Carol and Louise were heading in the direction of the GE facility nearest them upon leaving the scene. Were these crafts flying back home after being spotted?

Is it possible these events are all connected? Many UFO believers are convinced the government has been working in tandem with alien beings for many decades. Is it possible this partnership has been backed by several corporations across the nation, among them General Electric? It could be coincidence, of course. But, there seems to be enough evidence to support the theory.

4

So, on that night back in 1993, did Officers Graham and Downs just happen to stumble onto something they weren't supposed to see? Was there yet another unexplained light or saucer hovering above GE? These questions might never be answered. But even if all of this is far-reaching conspiracy nonsense, the truth remains that something odd did happen over GE that night in Louisville. An illuminated object of some kind engaged Louisville Air Patrol in an aggressive fashion, dodging around them and shooting fireballs. Four credible persons witnessed the incident, and each of them told practically the same tale. It's difficult to push something like that aside.

THE LOUISVILLE ALIEN, SPRING-HEELED JACK

When most people think of London murders, Jack the Ripper is the madman that comes to mind. While the Whitechapel serial killer is by far the most notorious, there are legends of another London lunatic that have grabbed the imaginations of folklorists. This killer predates the Ripper, and his name is also Jack. Just as elusive but even more bizarre, many believed this terror to be more than a man, but some sort of monster who breathed fire and could leap over buildings. They called him, Spring-heeled Jack.

Sightings of Jack allegedly began in the late 1700s. According to a letter written to the *Sheffield Times* in 1808, Jack had been bouncing around the streets of London for many years. In 1837, a man walking one night allegedly claimed that he saw a muscular man with pointed ears and glowing red eyes easily leap a cemetery fence and land directly in front of him. Not long after this incident, a woman named Polly Adams was found in the street with her blouse ripped from her body. She described a man with the same appearance accosting her, tearing off her blouse, and touching her with cold, corpse-like hands. These are unofficial reports.

Officially, Jack's first sighting was in 1837 when a woman by the name of Mary Stevens was attacked while walking along Cut Throat Lane on her way to Lavender Hill. As she was returning from a visit to her parents at Battersea, a tall, dark man leaped from the shadows, wrapped his arms around her, and commenced to kiss her wildly. As she struggled against him, he laughed hysterically. When she screamed, the attacker leaped away.

It is rumored that the following evening, the same man jumped into the middle of the road and caused an approaching carriage to veer off its path. He then bounded over a nine-foot wall without touching it and vanished into the night. A few days later, police arrived at a scene where Jack had been spotted, and they found very deep ruts in the mud, as if someone had jumped from a great height. They noticed that the impression on the ground

6

suggested that there was some kind of gadget attached to the heel. This supposed account has led to the theory that Jack was a man with springs on his shoes.

There were many more sightings over the next few years. Jack was accosting women, smacking men around, causing traffic issues, and inciting fear and hysteria in the populace. His legend was growing and developing all manner of odd descriptions. Some said this leaping man had bat-like wings, wore a cape, was pale and ghost-like, attacked them with long claws, and hands as hard as steel before jumping away high into the night. Some were speculating that he was a ghost while others claimed he was a shape-shifting monster. Most people laughed these accounts off as being nothing more than ghost stories. Nonetheless, these reports earned him the name, Spring-heeled Jack.

In February of 1838, the jumper struck again. Late in the evening, the doorbell rang at the home of a young woman named Jane Alsop. When Alsop opened the door, a cloaked man suddenly threw back his shroud to reveal white clothing that looked to be very tight oilskin. As strange as this incident was, it became even more bizarre when the man began to breathe blue and white fire at her face while slashing at her with razor-sharp claws. Alsop's sister rushed into the room and scared off the attacker before he inflicted any serious damage.

A man by the name of Thomas Millbank was arrested and tried for the crime, but was released due to Alsop's claim that her attacker was breathing fire, and Millbank, of course, could not do that. However, he had been found wearing white overalls, and police found that he had dropped a great coat and a candle outside the building.

An eighteen-year-old woman by the name of Lucy Scales had her own encounter with the jumping mini-dragon while she was walking with her sister in Limehouse. A figure leaped at her from the shadows of a nearby alley and started breathing fire into her face. Lucy screamed and the attacker fled. This incident left Scales in fits for several hours.

Many more sightings of the mysterious assailant occurred over the next few decades. His description took on new qualities with each report, such as his high-pitched laughter and large black boots. Witnesses continued to marvel at his inhuman leaping ability. They said he could clear walls without touching them, jump upon roofs of large houses, and quickly travel across town by leaping from rooftop to rooftop.

Sightings became more widespread, even if they were less frequent. A report from Northamptionshire described him as having horns and red eyes. He allegedly started attacking mail coaches in East Anglia, too. He supposedly tossed a prostitute off a bridge in 1845, in front of several witnesses. We could find no details explaining why witnesses believed Jack perpetrated this act. Perhaps the assailant leapt into the air before tossing the prostitute into the water. In 1847, a man named Captain Finch was arrested for attacking two women while wearing a skin coat, skullcap, horns, and mask.

An interesting incident occurred in 1855 after a hard snowfall in London. Albert Brailsford, headmaster of Topsham School in Devon, woke on February 8th to the sight of hoof prints in the snow. However, upon closer examination, Brailsford found some very odd details about these prints. First, they appeared to come not from a quadruped, but something bipedal. The prints were only eight inches apart and appeared to be about four inches in diameter. It looked as though they were in a straight line, as if whoever made them had been hopping along. He said they looked to have been branded into the snow, which would suggest they were made by something hot. From there, Brailsford and some of his friends decided to follow the tracks and see where they led. The prints stopped right in front of a large wall. The snow on top of the wall was not disturbed. It was as if the creator of the prints had jumped straight up over the wall.

The most sensational Jack account may have been in 1872, when reports claimed that he jumped down into a small squad of soldiers and slapped one of them in the face. This angered the soldier, so he took out his gun and shot Jack. Allegedly, the shot, though it connected, had no effect. It fact, it angered him. He then chased the soldiers around, spraying his blue and white flames at them. He stuck around for a few more days, pestering them with his antics. Eventually, a mob formed nearby and tried to capture him. He fled, and some of the people claimed to have shot him but to no avail. Jack kept running and spitting out fire before finally jumping to safety, out of sight. Not long after, there was a report that a couple of villagers had cornered Jack on a roof and shot him, but he leaped away unharmed.

England, it seems, is not the only nation that was terrorized by this bouncing boogeyman. In 1880, the same year Jack the Ripper was making his kills in London, Spring-heeled Jack allegedly came to Louisville. On July 28th, 1880, a man described as a "tall, thin weirdo" appeared in what is now known as Old Louisville, attacking women on the streets.

Reports claim that this person was leaping through the streets, tearing clothes off women. Many witnesses alleged to have seen him, and described him as having superhuman leaping abilities, jumping over carriages and onto rooftops to avoid capture. Though this Jack did not have red eyes, horns, nor did he breathe fire, it was said he wore a cape, helmet, and had a light glowing from his chest. It is also believed Jack bounded through Butchertown, as well, since one report stated he vanished behind some large haystacks after jumping over them. Some described Jack has having flown into Louisville on some machine that had peddles and propellers. According to the reports, he peddled his way through the dark skies of Downtown, shortly before and after these attacks occurred.

There has been much speculation as to whom and/or what Jack was through the years. Many people remain skeptical, believing Jack to have been nothing more than a common man with some very inventive methods of attack. The subsequent reports that followed the first two are believed to have been copycats, others a product of mass hysteria. Some say Jack was a nobleman by the name of Henry Beresford, Third Marquis of Waterford, who passed away in 1859. Beresford was known as the "Mad Marquis" due to his drunkenness and wild behavior. The biggest problem with this accusation is that there is zero evidence linking him to the Jack incidents.

The counterpoint to the claim that Jack was human is that the leaping abilities would have been impossible in such times. Many decades later, Nazi paratroopers who put springs in their boot heels in order to achieve better jumping abilities all ended up with broken ankles. Skeptics then insist that the additional attributes that made Jack superhuman were imagined. They argue his origins grew from stories about ghosts stalking the streets of London in the early 19th century. These "ghosts" were pale and humanlike, and they preyed upon those who walked the streets alone in the dark of night. These stories became a part of local lore and some say that it is what gave rise to the myth of Spring-heeled Jack.

Those who believe his existence to be otherworldly have other theories. Some say he was a demon summoned into our world by occult practitioners. But, one of the most common explanations is that he was extraterrestrial. Many believe that the descriptions of Jack—the red eyes, pointy ears, the pale skin, the long, spindly claws, the ability to leap and breathe fire—point to him being a visitor from another planet.

Regarding the leaping ability, it is believed that the creature, or creatures, we know as Spring-heeled Jack came from a planet that had a higher gravity than ours, which gave him that extraordinary vertical. Those who subscribe to this theory also believe this could explain his high-pitched laughter. Since our atmosphere would have seemed thin to him, it very well could have made him dizzy and somewhat excitable, which could have led to his riotous cackling and outlandish behavior. The eyes, they explain, could have been reflective due to him being from a darker planet where there is not as much light. His ability to breathe fire would have been either a bioelectric shock that his kind used to stun their victims, or some sort of phosphor lighted by his bioluminescence, which would explain why no one was actually burned by his perceived flames.

Accounts of Jack continued into the 20th century, across England and even into the states. In 1953, three Houston residents spotted a tall man in a black cape, skin-tight pants, and quarter-length boots leaping through town. They claim that he jumped into a Pecan tree, where he stayed in plain view for several minutes before a rocket-shaped UFO shot from across the street and took him away into the sky.

Naturally, there are those who say that even these reports are fabricated, and that no one in the 1800s, save for a few of the documented cases, ever reported encountering anyone like this. They say that while there were accounts stating a strange man was running around town accosting women, all of the additional sensationalism was embellished, and these embellishments grew into a very colorful super-villain story.

But there is no true evidence to support this explanation, and thus the believers keep believing. According to a few sources, Spring-heeled Jack did make his way to Old Louisville, and he was called the Demon Leaper. Was this the same individual? Did he fly across the ocean to our little corner of the world and cause a stir? It's quite possible. It could have been a copycat, or it could have not happened at all.

Let's just say for a minute that at least most of these accounts are true, and that this strange being did find himself bouncing around the streets of Louisville, making unwanted advances on women. The alien theories are definitely interesting points to consider. It could be why he had the gyroscope, if he did indeed have that. To the open-minded believer in the extraterrestrial, this is a fascinating possibility, and very intriguing addition to the encyclopedia of Kentucky alien encounters.

P1* Drawing of Spring-heeled Jack by unknown artist

CLOSE ENCOUNTERS WITH THE KELLY CREATURES

One of the most famous alien encounters, not only in Kentucky, but also in all of UFOlogy, is the Kelly-Hopkinsville Encounter of 1955. Also dubbed the Hopkinsville Goblins Case and the Kelly Green Men Case, this extraterrestrial incident occurred on August 21st, 1955 near Kelly and Hopkinsville in southwestern Kentucky.

On the evening of the aforementioned date, around 11pm, residents of the Sutton and Taylor family farmhouse near Kelly came into the police station and claimed they had been holding off small alien creatures with gunfire since dusk. During the family dinner, Billy Ray Taylor went out to the well around 7pm to retrieve some water and noticed a bright light flash across the sky. Several accounts claim that Billy Ray said the light was a flying saucer that landed behind a distant tree line. Other reports insist he did not say this and that he only said he saw a light shoot across the sky and disappear behind some trees.

After the light passed, the invasion began. The family heard strange noises around the property; the dogs nearby were barking, and then Billy Ray and Elmer Sutton saw the creatures emerge from the shadowy trees. They shot the first one that came into view and the others soon charged. The two men opened fire, but it did not affect their assailants. Instead, each shot ricocheted off the creatures with a sound like bullets striking a metal bucket. The creatures began floating to the ground and flying around the property, dodging bullets, ascending into trees, and escaping to the rooftops. One creature grabbed one of the men by the hair before he was able to retreat into the house.

By the time the men had exhausted their ammunition, the families decided these creatures were aliens. They had large, glowing eyes, antennas, claw-like hands, and were about three-feet in height. The children in the house took refuge beneath their beds as the aliens kept peeking in windows and appearing in doorways. It was estimated that there were anywhere between twelve and fifteen creatures.

Mrs. Lankford, who was renting the house, encouraged everyone to calm down, pointing out that the creatures, even though they seemed hostile, had not actually harmed anyone. Her suggestion was that they drive to the police station, and so they did.

This report concerned local authorities not because they believed aliens had attacked, but because they feared the shootout had been between neighbors. Five state troopers, four city police officers, four military police from nearby Fort Campbell, and three deputy sheriffs rode out to the house to investigate. They found spent shells lying about the property, doors and windows severely damaged by gunfire, but no sign of the alleged creatures. The only bit of evidence some say could have been leftover from the aliens was a glowing green substance on one of the fences. But this substance was found to be foxfire, a bioluminescent fungus that often grows on decayed wood.

The following day, two officers returned to the farmhouse to check up on the families only to find them gone. Neighbors said they had packed up and left because the creatures returned around 3:30 in the morning. Though they had not resumed the gunfight, they claimed that the creatures were scratching at the windows and walking along the roof. Other than Elmer and Billy Ray, the occupants of the home included Glennie Lankford and her children Lonnie, Charlton, and Mary; Elmer's wife Vera, Alene and J.C. Sutton, Alene's brother O.P. Baker, and Billy Ray's wife June. Each one of them had fled the home and decided to spend some time in Evansville, IN.

The incident received widespread press coverage, first local and then national. Many of the stories published by the newspapers, in subsequent books, and reported on radio and television were often inconsistent with the details. Some were accused of embellishment and outright fabrication. The alleged descriptions of the creatures, along with how the events unfolded, supposedly differed from what Billy Ray and the rest of the families originally stated. The story has always remained very muddled because of these inconsistencies.

The claim that the US Air Force got involved has been denied several times. Some have written that the Air Force studied the incident and then deemed it "unidentified". But in truth, the Air Force was never involved and they have labeled this case as a hoax in Project Blue Book.

Although the incident was eventually called the "Kelly Green Men Case," the Sutton family had not initially described them as being green. Certain newspapers later added that attribute. Despite that, this case popularized the phrase, "little green men". The term had appeared in science fiction prior to this, but after the Kelly-Hopkinsville Case, newspapers and radio shows were using the expression often.

Skepticism surrounds the case. Psychologists and academics believe that what the Suttons thought were alien creatures were actually great horned owls. Great horned owls are nocturnal, have glowing eyes, high pointy ears, are silent during flight, and will aggressively defend their nests if they feel threatened; they can also be as tall as two feet and have great wingspans. They are the second biggest owl living in North America.

Skeptics have attributed the light Billy Ray saw streak across the sky to a meteor shower that took place near Kentucky that night. Assertions that Billy Ray claimed to have seen a flying saucer land near the property have been deemed inaccurate. This statement does not appear in the original police reports.

Those who believe the aggressors to be aliens cite the longevity of the claim, as well as the number of eyewitnesses. Those who knew Elmer Sutton say that he was a stable, no-nonsense kind of man who would not make this up. They also point out that the family has never attempted to capitalize on the incident. Others have countered this by saying that they don't believe Elmer and the others were lying. They don't doubt the families were genuinely frightened by what they believed were aliens, they just think they were wrong.

It truly is hard to say for certain what these Hopkinsville Goblins were. Some certainly believe they were aliens. Others of course believe they were not. We're not saying we believe with certainty they were alien creatures, though they very well could have been. If there is a non-paranormal explanation, we believe they were possibly great horned owls. But if they weren't, then the Sutton and Taylor families really did have a close encounter with the Kelly Creatures.

Alien or not, the town of Hopkinsville celebrates this incident on its anniversary with their Kelly Little Green Men Days festival. It is a great event to check out if you are an alien enthusiast.

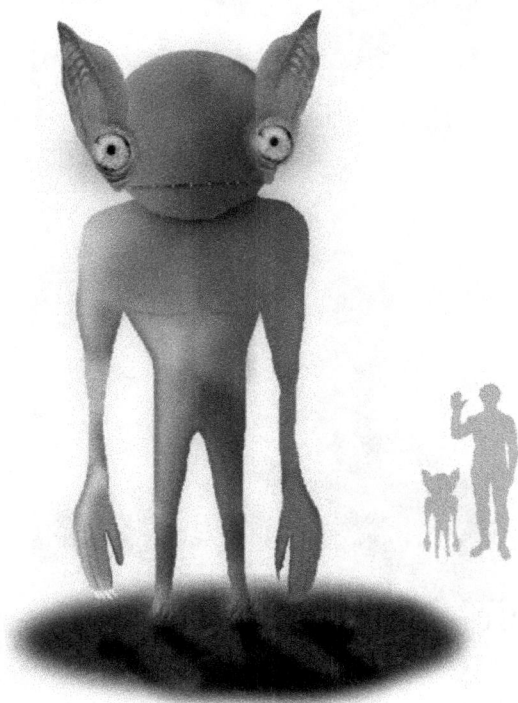

P2* Drawing of Hopkinsville Goblin by Tim Bertelink

*P3: Great Horned Owl, photo by Billy Hunt

IT'S RAINING MEAT!

On March 3rd 1876, small chunks of flesh, ranging from to two-to-four square inches, rained down from the sky over a 100-by-50-yard area. This incident is known as the Kentucky Meat Shower and it happened over Olympia Springs in Bath County (ironically enough). It was a peculiar occurrence and quite disturbing for those involved. The event was reported in the *New York Times* and *Scientific American*, as well as other publications.

A woman by the name of Mrs. Crouch was out on her porch that sunny afternoon making soap when the grisly chunks of flesh began slapping the ground all around her, causing her alarm. There was no rain accompanying the meat shower. Mrs. Crouch's husband, Allen, joined her side, and they watched for several minutes as the meat rained down around them. Once the shower had passed, the sky remained just as clear as it had been prior to the strange event. They believed the meat shower was a sign from God.

A man by the name of Harrison Gill visited the Crouch property the following day and saw bits of meat sticking to fences, resting on the roof, and lying scattered about the grounds. Enough had fallen to fill a wagon. The general belief was that the meat was beef. But after word spread, two other men unknown to the Crouches showed up and asked to taste it. After doing so, they concluded that it was either mutton or venison. A local hunter by the name of B.F. Ellington ate some and declared that it was bear meat. But the mystery was not what matter of animal the meat came from, but what had caused it to fall from the sky.

The first explanation came from a man named Leopold Brandeis who, after studying some of the specimens, said that it was not actually meat at all, but something called nostoc, which is a cyanobacteria covered by a gelatinous substance. Whenever it rains, nostoc swells up into a jelly-like mass and drops from the sky. The particular breed of nostoc in the Bath

County area was flesh-colored when swollen, and it tasted like chicken or frog-legs. It was Brandeis's opinion that this nostoc had been floating on the breeze unnoticed and then blew up when it rained and fell upon the Crouch property.

The problem with this theory is that there had been no rain when this happened, which debunked Brandeis's explanation. So, he gave some samples to the Newark Scientific Association for further analysis.

The Newark Scientific Association then determined it was not nostoc, and that it was indeed meat. The results from their analysis concluded that two of the pieces were actually lung tissue from either a human infant or a horse; three more specimens were determined to be muscle, and the other two were cartilage.

Some locals blamed this incident on turkey vultures. Their theory is that one bird started vomiting up its food and then the others followed suit, which is customary behavior for their breed. Dr. L.D. Kastenbine supported this theory as being the likeliest explanation. Vomiting is a turkey vulture's defense mechanism when it is threatened. They can projectile vomit for up to ten feet, which can often dispel any threatening animals. Kastenbine said that the most likely scenario was that the vultures started vomiting from a great height, causing the meat to scatter in the wind. The variety of tissue that was found supports this theory. The pressure from the drop and regurgitation could be why the meat had a dry, flat texture. Nine days later, this incident happened again, only it was over London, England.

While the vomiting vulture theory sounds like the most plausible, and is certainly the best rational explanation we'll probably every get for this phenomenon, others think there may be otherworldly ties to this occurrence. There are those who believe this mysterious meat rain is linked to extraterrestrial activity and they point to the fact that so many incidents similar to this have occurred around the world for more than a century.

On August 17th, 1841, two servants working in a tobacco field in Lebanon, Tennessee came in from their work around 1pm and reported that blood had rained down upon them. They were working the field and heard a strange rattling sound that they compared to the sound of rain or hail, and looked around to see that blood was coming out of a red cloud passing overhead. When the field was investigated, droplets of blood were found on the tobacco leaves; small chunks of meat were discovered in the area, as well. The meat shower covered an area roughly forty-to-sixty-yards wide and six-to-eight-hundred-yards long. Though it was decided that the meat was from an unknown animal, the blood was said to be more like a paste.

There was also an incident in Fayetteville, North Carolina on February 15th, 1850 near the home of Thomas Clarkson. A shower of blood, flesh, liver, and brains covered an area roughly thirty yards wide and three-hundred in length. The event also left blood running down leaves on nearby trees. Their three children were outside when the shower began. As the meat fell around them, they ran to the house screaming, "There is meat falling!" Neighbors about 150 yards away witnessed this event. They claimed that the meat fell from a red cloud that was passing over, and they could smell the scent of blood in the air.

Slovenia also felt the brunt of this phenomenon on October 20th, 1851 when meat fell mysteriously upon an army station near Benicia. A man known as Major Allen noticed the shower first when he was struck by a piece of falling meat. He then watched the shower for another three minutes. He described the chunks ranging in size from a pigeon's egg to an orange, some even weighing up to three ounces. The entire rain covered land about three-hundred-yards long and eighty-yards-wide. It was said there was about two-and-a-half to five bushels of flesh altogether. The meat appeared to be beef, was boneless, but showed plenty of muscle and vessels. No birds were spotted in the air and the sky was clear.

California experienced two meat rains in 1869. One occurred in March in San Francisco, where chunks of meat fell from the sky and pelted a man while he was walking down the street. He collected several specimens over about five acres. Another occurred in Los Angeles County on August 1st, 1869. A shower of what appeared to be freshly torn meat, some merely fine particles and others in stripes as long as eight inches, fell across two acres of farmland in Los Nietos. There was no analysis conducted to determine what exactly the meat was, but there was little doubt that it was flesh and blood.

On February 25th, 1884, Mrs. Kit Lasater was walking home in New Hope, North Carolina when she heard a hard rain starting to fall. When she looked up, she saw only a clear sky above her. When she looked back down, she saw a splattering of blood all around her. It had drenched the ground and the nearby trees in a roughly sixty-foot radius. Several samples were collected and sent to Dr. F.P. Venable and all but one was concluded to be blood.

On August 27th, 1968, a shower of blood and meat fell for several minutes over a square kilometer between Cocpava and Sao Jose dos Campos in Brazil. The chunks were spongy and violet, varying in sizes between five and twenty centimeters. There were no reports of storms, birds, or aircrafts in the sky at the time.

In 2016, blood and boneless meat rained down on the Argentinean village of Picun Leufu, covering about fifty meters of land. A man was tending to animals in his fields when he heard the meat begin falling around him like hail. From where he stood in the field, he could hear it hitting the house. His wife, who was in the nursery at the time, heard the rain and believed it to be hail too until she saw flesh and blood on the roof. No one saw any aircrafts in the area and could not explain the incident.

As you can see, Kentucky is not alone in this long history of peculiar meat showers. Alien theorists point to the number of times this has happened and the peculiar nature of each incident as being too coincidental to be ruled out as vulture vomit. Could there be a link to these meat showers and the mysterious airship sightings of the late 1800s? The dates the ships were spotted don't entirely match up with the meat showers, but they are close enough together to warrant consideration.

The most noted airship sightings began in California in 1896 and spread east through 1897. But in 1887, there were allegedly many reports of strange craft sightings along the East Coast. In 1880, there is the incident discussed in the previous chapter about Spring-heeled Jack, when a man was seen flying into Louisville on a gyroscope-like device, using his hands and feet to steer it. Not likely that incident would have anything to do with the meat, though. Even as far back as 1868, an unexplained airship was spotted over Copiapo, Chile. This could be a reaching theory, but it does seem strange that these sightings would happen not long after the meat showers.

Even though livestock mutilation didn't become a concern until the late 1900s, it had been happening sporadically for many centuries. Maybe these meat showers resulted from that. To those who believe aliens are involved with these blood rains, it could be that cattle were mutilated in alien crafts and their remains then tossed away. UFO sightings became more frequent in the late 1900s, when mutilations became prevalent. Perhaps the aliens had decided to alter their methods and view the creatures in their natural habitats when experimenting on them.

Could it be that the Kentucky meat shower was just one incident in a long timeline of alien cattle abduction and mutilation, or was this incident truly just turkey vultures puking up dinner?

*P4: Specimen from the Kentucky meat shower, by Bec Crew; sample belongs to the Arthur Byrd Cabinet at Transylvania University

COAL TRAIN BATTLES THE SPACECRAFT

On April 3rd, 2006, an anonymous person filed a controversial report stating they were working aboard a coal train to Shelbiana, KY when it collided with a UFO somewhere in Paintsville. According to the report, the incident occurred about four years prior to the filing. This story circulated around the UFO community and quickly garnered much attention from both skeptics and believers.

The collision happened around 2:47 on the morning of January 14th, 2002; the train was en route from Russell, approaching a bend near milepost CMG 42, when the poster and the conductor saw multiple bright lights ahead. Thinking this was an oncoming train located on the other track, they turned off their lights so as not to blind the other crew. As they drew nearer to the lights, the onboard computer systems began to malfunction and both of the locomotives died. Then, the alarms on the train began to ring.

The area they were passing through is called the Wild Kingdom because of the various breeds of animals that live there. On one side of the dual tracks was the river; on the other was a hill. After the alarm started going off, the poster and conductor saw at least three floating crafts to the left of the train, scanning the river with their lights. The first craft they encountered was hovering about ten to twelve feet above the tracks. It was metallic and silver, about ten feet tall and twenty in length, with no windows and multicolored lights at the bottom of it.

Due to both engines being dead, the locomotive rounded the bend silently. Whoever was in command of the floating object did not realize the train was bearing down on them. In seconds, the train collided with the UFO at about 30mph with 16,000 tons of trailing cars behind them. The initial impact grazed the lead unit, but it sent the craft sailing, causing it to take a long slice out of their trailing unit and first two coal cars. After this, the other crafts disappeared.

When the electricity had gone out, the emergency brakes initiated and the train stopped about two miles after the crash. Once the locomotive was stationary, the electricity returned and the workers were able to contact their dispatcher in Jacksonville, FL to alert him of the collision. The dispatcher then instructed them to inspect the train, assess the damage, and determine if it would be able to pull into milepost CMG 60 located in the Paintsville yard, which was no longer operational.

After inspection, the two men discovered that the cab of the rear locomotive was decimated and smoking. The two cars that followed the cab were also badly damaged, but looked like they could make it to Paintsville yard.

The train pulled into CMG 60 a little after five-in-the-morning. The overhead lights around the yard were out, but there were lights at the other end of the track, which the men assumed were emanating from vehicles belonging to railroad officials. Once they stopped and disembarked to unload the grips from the wounded train, they heard what they thought was a bunch of railroad workers coming towards them.

The ruckus of chatter and slamming doors preceded the approach of men in suits. The suited men came upon the poster and conductor and began searching the locomotives. A man who called himself Ferguson greeted them and shook their hands, asking them to follow him to the former yard office. Once inside, a group of unidentified men began asking many questions. After the interrogation was complete, the poster and conductor were told they would have to be medically cleared before they could leave. They requested to speak to their trainmaster and/or railroad foreman, but were denied these requests, and the interrogators confiscated the conductor's cell phone.

After a few hours, they were released from the yard office and led to another railroad vehicle. As they crossed the yard, they noticed the two locomotives and two coal cars were separated from the rest of the train and under a large tent four tracks away. Before the other men led them to the railroad vehicle, they were told that their silence regarding this event would be appreciated, as this was a matter of national security.

The vehicle took them to Martin, KY where they were questioned further and then drug tested. After the two men were cleared of any drug use, they were sent to Shelbiana to rest. About eight hours later, they were put back to work on another train headed back to Russell. As they passed the location of the crash, they did not see the locomotives, the cars, or the train. None of the men or their vehicles were there; not even the tent remained. It was as if nothing out of the ordinary had occurred at CMG 42.

This incident has come under scrutiny from the UFO community and its debunkers. Many have asked for the train car numbers, and want to know if reports of them being damaged or missing exist. Most of all, they want to know who filed this report.

Naturally, some think it's a hoax – a fake report filed for a gag. With the lack of documentation of not only the incident, but the trip as well, and with no name attached to the report, it is very logical to assume this was a faux encounter. Some have pointed out the unlikelihood of a 16,000-pound train stopping two miles after the emergency brakes hit while having travelled at 30mph. It is also unlikely that riding at this speed, the train would have been silent with the emergency brakes engaged. The metal-on-metal sound of the wheel flanges grinding against the rails would have been loud enough to alert anyone of the train's approach. Also, as some counterpoints explain, the brakes would have slowed the train quickly, and it would not have hit the craft at 30mph, more like fifteen or twenty.

Other details in the report have been challenged. The area the train was passing through is called the Big Sandy Subdivision, which has a speed limit of 30mph for cars over 14,000 pounds. The Big Sandy has many curves, and the speed limit around these curves is reduced to 20 or 25mph. Trains as big as the one described in this report would struggle getting up to 30mph around these curves.

The area known as Wild Kingdom is said to be ten miles south of the site of the crash. The light that they saw around the curve could have very well been the light of cars passing on a state road located next to the tracks. In this area, many vehicles have bright off-road lights they like to shine down this dark stretch of road at night.

Also, trying to drive the train into the yard after the collision would have been against protocol. At the very least, the conductor would have been required to walk the entire train and perform brake tests. This train has been estimated at being about a mile long, and that would have taken an hour at the least to properly inspect, most likely longer due to the environment, not to mention the fact that coal would have littered the area, which would have made walking the length of the train even more difficult. It's also been pointed out that the train would not have even been permitted to move until a trainmaster came out and gave the all clear after assessing the damage. But, if the train did go ahead and continue on to Paintsville yard, it would have had to travel at about eight or nine miles-per-hour, which, after all of this, would have had clocked its arrival in at around 7am.

Furthermore, the conductor would have been on the radio with someone at a post, getting clear signals or traffic reports. The idea that he never spoke to anyone until after the crash has been pointed to as a major flaw in the story.

However, those who believe this report to be true point to the level of detail, and how it reads like a genuine report written by someone with an obvious working knowledge of railroad work and lingo, and not someone just making up a story on the fly. Railroad workers have challenged many of the counterpoints listed above, stating that those who argue the report is a fake know very little about railroad work, the area the train was in, and the protocols or how tightly they are followed. They have offered counterarguments debunking these explanations. Some who claim to know the men in the report have vouched for the coal spillage and for the men as well, saying that they did indeed hit something, even if they don't know what it was they hit.

They also ask why the men at Paintsville yard questioned the poster and conductor, took the conductor's cell phone, asked for their silence, and then made the evidence disappear. The conclusion is that this was a genuine alien encounter and the mystery men who appeared after the train's arrival in the Paintsville yard wanted to keep the incident quiet.

Others believe this to be a genuine report, but not an alien encounter. Instead, they believe the train struck a Cypher UAV, an unmanned craft operated hands free belonging to the US Marine Corps. This machine has been blamed for many UFO sightings, as it is disk shaped, silent, and can hover in one spot. The original model fits the description given by the poster, with its sensor standing several feet above the body, which would give it the appearance of being around ten feet tall. If these military search drones were operating under an electromagnetic countermeasures condition, that would have caused some electronic anomalies aboard the train. This explanation seems not only high plausible, but very likely.

If this craft is what the train hit, then that could explain the men who took over the situation. That would explain why they were there so soon after the crash, and why they would request the two keep silent because they wouldn't want word of the then-new technology getting out.

It is also very likely that these men, whom the poster claims to have not known, really were CSX workers that wanted to clean the incident up and make sure the men were fine. Even though it seems odd that they wouldn't allow them to speak with their foreman or trainmaster, and that they would confiscate the cell phone, it very well could be a simple measure of CSX protocol.

Besides, if aliens have crafts capable of flying here from other worlds, that implies they possess highly advanced technology. If an earthling locomotive moving 30mph could take out one of their crafts, it doesn't say much about their ability to wield that technology. Perhaps these crafts were new models.

In 2010, there was a UFO sighting reported to have happened in the area not long before the train collision took place. A firefighter and paramedic from Paintsville were driving home after their shift and saw a large light zigzagging across the road. The light was at a height level with the treetops as it passed over top of them. Two more emerged suddenly on either side of the car. The car began to malfunction; it didn't quit, but lights started flashing and the gauges started going crazy. The lights soon passed on and everything returned to normal.

If this report is authentic, then it seems the strange crafts were in the area around the time of the collision. While that doesn't mean they were alien craft, as they still could have been the UAVs, it does corroborate the poster's report. It seems to us that the evidence points to the collision actually having happened, even if the details may or may not have been a little off. Does it point to extraterrestrial involvement? Not necessarily, but that doesn't mean it wasn't a close encounter.

This is certainly a muddled account with several conflicts. Whether or not the craft in question belonged to visitors from another world, it is still an interesting case. Would it really be necessary for the government to resort to such extreme measures after the accident, if those men were indeed government agents? If this were merely a search drone, would they really need to act so urgently and secretively about it? Possibly. But that doesn't account for the multicolored lights at the bottom of the craft.

Either way, the poster will no doubt always remember this event. They will also always remember the exact time it happened, because when all the electronics on board went haywire, the poster's watch froze at 2:47am, and has remained that way ever since.

AREA 51 OF THE SOUTH

Madison County is an area of Kentucky known for UFO activity, especially near the Bluegrass Army Depot (or the BGAD), which lies between Richmond and Berea. Opening in 1942, the BGAD is more than 14,000 acres of woods and open fields and is used mainly for the creation and storage of chemical weapons and other munitions. It is also a munitions dumping ground, and a place for general repairs and weapons testing. At least, that is the official function listed for BGAD's operations. Some believe it is also used for classified purposes, specifically involving alien technology.

Rumors state that the depot is actually a testing ground for this alien technology. Allegedly, an alien craft crashed near there long ago and has been stored underground and reverse-engineered at the facility to develop advanced weaponry and crafts. This reverse engineering supposedly lead to the development of the Stealth Bomber and other aircrafts, including one that is invisible, and has a hull that acts as both camera and monitor, projecting images from one side of the plane to the other.

UFO sightings in the area are abundant. Every style of spacecraft has been seen near the depot. The always-famous flying saucers have been seen, the notorious black triangles, and the cigar-shaped ships. Folks have also reported mysterious lights hovering in the sky over and around the BGAD.

Unmarked black helicopters are often seen in the vicinity, as well. Some reports state that the choppers are either coming from or going into the depot. Witnesses say that some are Blackhawks while others seem to be more advanced. These vehicles have been seen flying to and from the directions of Ft. Campbell as well as the Central Kentucky Regional Airport, located in Richmond.

The BGAD is heavily guarded and secluded from civilization, such is the case with most military outposts. This compounds the belief that super-

31

secret otherworldly technology is stored there. But, it could just be because such dangerous weaponry lies within the massive buildings behind the tall fences topped with razor wire. Chemical weapons are not to be taken lightly. There have been several instances of sarin and mustard gas leaks occurring at the BGAD. Both substances can be lethal, so it's no wonder they don't want people wandering in and out of the compound.

Some also question why the depot has cattle on property. The reason given for this is that it's a way of warning personnel of any chemical leaks. The effect the chemical had on the cattle would be indication of the leak, and the army would then be able to respond. This could help avoid a situation similar to what occurred in 1979 when forty residents near BGAD were hospitalized after a cloud of gas burst in the air.

Due to the United States ending its chemical weapons programs in the 1960s, more than 90% of the nation's chemical weapons have been destroyed. The Bluegrass Army Depot is one of two facilities left that contains them, with more than nine-hundred bunkers full. Undoubtedly, a time will come for the weapons there to be destroyed, it's just uncertain when it will happen. When it does happen, what effect the loss of the weapons will have on the facility as well as the county is unknown. It could lead to lost jobs, which would no doubt have a negative impact on the local economy. If this does occur, then the BGAD could be used as a historical site since some of the area is the Battle of Richmond battlefield, of which they host an annual reenactment on property. A portion of Daniel Boone's trace is located on the depot, as well. They already allow tours of the facility, perhaps if the weapons were gone, they could expand that tour and include the other historic locations.

Maybe they could even capitalize on the UFO rumors, as well. Could you imagine the turnout if they started offering UFO tours, having an alien festival and gift shop, and even hosting alien story hour? We imagine there would be a few lucrative uses for the Bluegrass Army Depot if the chemical weapons were to be removed.

A SKY FULL OF SQUARES

Speaking of the Bluegrass Army Depot, another phenomenon transpired near there in 1985. Residents in Berea reported seeing several large cubes floating in the sky. The numerous reports varied as to how large the objects appeared, but each account stated that they were cubes and not saucer-shaped.

Multiple witnesses, including a local forest ranger, saw one passing over the small town of Oneida, which lies roughly 60 miles to the southeast of Berea. Witnesses say they saw red lights on each side of it. They also reported it moving at varying speeds. Some say it was moving quickly, others say it was hovering very slowly.

Thirteen years later, in 1999, a sudden rash of cube sightings occurred in Richmond, which is only fourteen miles north of Berea. Some of these reports were contrary to the previously reported cube shapes. Some said the craft was flat with a square base, which gave it a cubic appearance when viewed from below. One eyewitness said he had seen them flying low and could identify a section on their underside where landing gear would emerge. He said he thought this was not an alien craft at all, but a man-made military plane on a test flight.

While the Bluegrass Army Depot is very near to these sightings, and for years has tested military craft, it makes sense to assume this flying object belongs to them even though there has been no connection made between the BGAD and the cubes. However, the many years of reported alien activity occurring in and around the depot leaves others to believe that these sightings are linked to extraterrestrials. Maybe even the ship reported in 1999 was not the same cube from the mid-80s, or perhaps a new version of it. Some ask how the presence of landing gear disqualified the possibility that the craft is alien. Aliens need to land their ships, too.

Whether or not these sightings were vehicles from another planet is open for speculation. But there were excessively many sightings in 85, 86, and 99 to claim this was a hoax. Something strange was certainly floating through the skies, and it was not a traditional plane, or even the usual UFO.

THE CREATURE, THE CRAFT, AND THE UNEXPLAINED LIGHTS

When two separate areas so close together have a history of strange phenomena, the possibility of their connection is worth exploring. That would be the case with Mt. Sterling and Sand Mountain. Sand Mountain has a long history of unexplained lights, while Mt. Sterling once had a rather prominent UFO sighting.

In June 1973, three men passing through Mt. Sterling claimed an alien spacecraft followed them to a friend's house. As they crossed into town around 5pm, they saw a massive ship emerge from behind an expanse of trees and begin hovering over their vehicle at a height of about a hundred feet. The discus craft had an array of colored lights flickering at different speeds across its body, made no sound, and contained no beams or spotlights.

According to the claim, they were not the only ones to see the UFO. As they drove into town, cars were stopping and people were standing on the street, looking up as the ship passed overhead. All over town, people were looking to the sky at this large prismatic saucer hovering over their streets. Once the men reached their destination, the saucer stopped. More people gathered to observe this strange spectacle. Minutes later, the craft rose into the air and vanished.

Despite the number of witnesses, some find this tale hard to believe. But it isn't as if the area near Mt. Sterling doesn't have other strange sightings. Located in the small city of Jeffersonville, KY, about eight miles south of Mt. Sterling, is Sand Mountain, which is allegedly haunted.

For decades, people have observed unexplained lights floating along the mountaintop. Many call them "ghost lights". Some speculate that these lights could be spirits from a graveyard located somewhere on the mountain. Others, however, think they may actually be intelligent, because they follow people and hover over certain areas before vanishing. These actions have led people to believe these lights may be of alien origin.

There is also a legend about a large white creature wandering the back roads and wooded areas of Sand Mountain. Some have described this creature as a massive quadruped that stalks the night, looking for people drifting through the hills. Others have said it is a tall, pale, alien creature with a round head and black eyes, and if it catches you, it will grab you with its spindly arms and take you into the mysterious lights where it lives.

Of course, who knows how much truth lies in such an interesting legend. This white creature could be any number of wild animals living in Sand Mountain. People have reported hearing strange noises, like screaming and shrieking, coming from the mountain at night. Most likely, these are bobcats. Who's to say that this alien monster isn't just one of these animals that have grown larger and more menacing with each telling of the story?

However, by this book's end, you will have read theories regarding the possibility of subterranean creatures existing here on Earth, and how their presence could be connected to many sightings of not only UFO and alien activity, but frightening creatures found in the underground places of the country. Enough reports of extraterrestrial events have occurred near caves, mineshafts, and mountains, that it leads one to believe that there is a connection. The creatures recorded and encountered by others through the years also scream and shriek, much like bobcats or other wild animals. Again, we will discuss that further in the book, but it could be that this white walker on Sand Mountain is one of these subterranean beings.

Then you have the phantom lights, reported countless times for more than a hundred years. What if the Sand Mountain creature is from another planet and it came here long ago on that strange craft spotted in 1973? The lights have been reported since the early 1900s, perhaps even before then, and we know how much strange activity was reported in Kentucky late in the 1800s. Maybe it is all connected. Maybe it's all just fantasy. For the alien and paranormal enthusiast—and no doubt the skeptic, too—it's all interesting.

THE STANFORD ABDUCTIONS

Other than sightings of flying crafts and strange lights, UFOlogy has many reports of alien abductions. Abductees often claim they were experimented on after being taken aboard an alien craft. There have been nearly 2000 reports of alien abductions, with those who survey such claims believing maybe five to six percent of them to be legitimate.

Kentucky is home to one very well documented abduction case. It occurred January 6th, 1976 in Stanford, KY. Three women—Mona Stafford, Louisa Smith, and Elaine Thomas—would have a terrifying encounter with a UFO that night.

Elaine and Louisa had joined Mona for dinner at the Redwood restaurant just south of Lancaster, some thirty-five miles from the town of Liberty where the three women lived. It was Mona's 36th birthday and they had decided to brave the thirty-eight degree weather to celebrate it. But what began as a night of celebration turned into a nightmare they would never forget.

The women finished their dinner and left the restaurant around 11:15pm. They got into Louisa's '67 Chevy Nova and travelled on Highway 78 on their way out of Stanford towards Hustonville. As the car sped along, they saw a bright red object appear suddenly in the sky. Mona was terrified, thinking it was an airplane engulfed in flames about to crash near them. Louisa became increasingly frightened as the object drew closer, and she lost control of the vehicle.

The automobile accelerated to 85mph, without Louisa pushing it to do so. In fact, she would later state that her foot was not even on the gas pedal. She was not one to drive fast anyway, and she was now yelling that she could not control the Nova. Thinking something had gone wrong with the steering, Mona, who was in the passenger seat, reached over and grabbed the wheel to try to straighten the vehicle out. However, she could not control the wheel, either. It was as if some other force had assumed command of the vehicle.

The women reported that the craft drew closer and followed behind them for several minutes. All the while, the car never deviated from its accelerated speed. Suddenly, the object moved to the left and descended, hovering near the driver side. This gave all three women the opportunity for an up-close view. When they issued their report, each woman described the craft as being large, metallic, and disk-shaped, domed at the top with a ring of red light circling its midsection. Underneath, they could see a yellow light blinking on the belly.

The UFO continued to ride beside them for several minutes before it shot ahead of them on the highway. After doing so, a bright, bluish-white light erupted from it, illuminating the interior of the car and filling it with a haze. The women's skin and eyes began to burn, and the last memory they said they had was of the car backing into a pasture in what they described as a "crazy manner".

Almost ninety minutes later, the three women found themselves back in the car, driving towards Liberty. They were upset and found that each of them had areas of their skin exposed, all with burning sensations. When they arrived at Louisa's house, they checked the clock and saw that it was now 1:20am. The thirty-five-mile trip that normally took about forty-five minutes had taken just over two hours.

Confused by this development, they went to the house of neighbor Lowell Lee and asked her for the time; Lee confirmed that it was indeed as late as they thought. Unsure of what to do, they called the police. The following day, they phoned the Navy recruiting station. Neither call yielded any assistance. The Navy recruiting station did pass along the report to a Lexington TV station, and the incident was soon a local headline.

Jerry Black of the Mutual UFO Network (MUFON) heard of the event and tried to contact the three women for an interview, but they were hesitant to relive the harrowing experience, or to have strangers visiting their homes. It took much persistence and empathy on Black's part to get the women to agree to the interview.

Accompanied by Mrs. Peggy Schnell, someone who had a lot of experience with abduction cases, Black headed to Liberty to meet with the women. During the first interview, some very important details emerged. It turned out the women had lost quite a bit of weight since the incident, and experienced unquenchable thirst. They also began chain-smoking, and were in great physical pain. They could not remember much of the event, much to their chagrin as they were hoping Black and Schnell would be able to help them. Mona said she lived in fear of the forgotten details, and was concerned that the other two women were on the verge of a psychological breakdown.

Louisa had experienced increasing difficulty completing her tasks at work. Mona suffered from a serious eye inflammation; however, she was mostly concerned about the events she could not remember. All three women were informed that they could undergo regressive hypnosis to learn what happened during that time.

It was obvious to investigators that the women were not making this up. They had the scars to prove it, physically and emotionally. Louisa carried a gray and pinkish half-dollar-sized blotchy scar on the nape of her neck. Weird things also started happening around her. The minute hand of her watch began to spin rapidly, and when she touched her alarm clock, it stopped working.

Her parakeet would not have anything to do with her after she returned home the night of the abduction. On that night, as soon as Louisa had walked through the door, the usually docile bird began screeching and flapping its wings wildly while bouncing around the cage. Investigators conducted a test with Louisa and other birds. Whenever anyone approached them, the birds acted normal. Whenever Louisa approached, they reacted very much the same way as her parakeet. Likewise, when others approached her parakeet, it behaved. The parakeet died two months later.

To all of those involved in the investigation, it was clear that this account was as solid as could be. The three women were reliable, mature, and respectable. They had not been drinking that night at Redwood, and they were clearly in a state of confusion and turmoil regarding this happening. They had not sought notoriety for it, only help. In fact, when Dr. Leo Sprinkle, a known UFOlogist, had agreed to come all the way from Wyoming to perform the regressive hypnosis on them, they initially refused, believing that time would heal all wounds.

Mona eventually agreed to the hypnosis. The first session yielded no answers. She was unable to get past the beginning where she believed the saucer to be a burning airliner hurtling through the night sky. After waking her from the hypnosis, Sprinkles advised Black that if he was going to ask Mona anymore questions to do so very carefully since she was still in a post-hypnotic state. Mona then moved away from the other women to lie down as Black turned his focus on the others.

One of the other interviewers began to show Mona drawings of extraterrestrials. No one had mentioned aliens yet during the investigation. Their reasons for avoiding the word were so they would not frighten nor influence the women. As the interviewer went through some drawings, Mona stopped them on one and exclaimed that the light she'd seen had been shaped like the creature's head. As she contemplated the image, fuzzy memories came to her, and she then professed that she saw a face that looked very much like the alien's in the drawing.

The investigators then determined that they had breached the lapse in time and concluded that abduction had transpired. However, it was several months before the investigation continued. During that time, investigators kept in touch with the women, but did not push them for answers. Mainly, they were concerned with the women's recovery. They still had physical complications and the fear and weight loss continued.

The investigation team also faced problems financing further research. Black found a solution when he contacted the *National Enquirer* and they agreed to finance the remaining investigations. A lie-detector test and regressive hypnosis would be conducted. If it was determined that an alien abduction had occurred, the *Enquirer* would get the exclusive rights to publish the story, for which the women would receive compensation. Black made the deal not just for the UFO research groups, but also out of concern for the women's health.

The next hypnosis session would take place on June 23rd at the Brown Hotel in Liberty, for which UFO researcher and member of the *National Enquirer* staff Bob Pratt would be present. Pratt was an honest man, despite the *Enquirer*'s spotty reputation. He had previously attempted to get information on the Stanford case, but could not due to the media blackout placed upon it.

Before the hypnosis began, Detective James Young of the Lexington Police Department conducted a polygraph test on each woman individually. Young was skeptical of UFO and alien claims. He came into the tests thinking the women were lying. Each test he conducted was lengthy, leaving nothing unturned. Once they were completed, an amazed Young declared that each woman had "breezed through" the tests. It was concluded there was no deception in their stories. They were not lying.

Now it was time for the hypnosis. Dr. Sprinkle put Louisa under that evening. All three women would receive two sessions the following day. It was reported that during each session, the fear and torment was clear on each woman's face. They were noticeably haunted by the experience.

The sessions resulted in the very answers the investigators were seeking. Between all sessions, the frightening details came together as the women subconsciously told their stories. At times, they would even reenact what happened to them by contorting and moving about.

The account recovered through hypnosis reports that the women were taken aboard the craft where the abductors commenced a variety of physical examinations on them, some of which were torturous. Often times, they were restrained in what they said were humiliating positions, though nothing sexual occurred. Louisa said her examination took place on a table; Mona's was in some sort of chair; Elaine was in a capsule with a device that she likened to a noose around her neck, which tightened if she tried to speak. All three recalled being scanned and having instruments used on them that caused great pain and pressure in their extremities. Mona and Elaine described having a warm liquid poured on their faces. Elaine recalled a bullet-tipped tube probing her chest.

The women could not provide a detailed description of the abductors, however. They mostly referred to them as shadowy people that floated by them. They all described "one eye" and "two eyes" that hovered above them. They all agreed that the beings communicated via telepathy because no mouths were visible.

Mona was able to provide a detailed description of an eye exam she endured. She said she recalled seeing a light at the end of a jagged tunnel that resembled a volcano, and spoke specifically of a bright purple eye that radiated rays like lightning. She remembered looking through that tunnel into a room that suddenly burst with light. In the center was a square table, and on that table lay a helpless woman undergoing examination at the hands of several small figures dressed in white. She did not recall if that woman had been Elaine or Louisa, or even herself.

41

Elaine recalled two-eyes in a round head shrouded in darkness. One eye was dark and the other a beautiful blue, surrounded by a blue membranous lid. She also stated that the captors were about four feet tall. Though Louisa stated she had seen shadowy figures, very much as the other two women described, she had apparently closed her eyes during the exams, afraid to see too much.

The verdict of the investigators was that these women did indeed see an unknown craft, and had been abducted by unidentified beings. If their testimonies, both under hypnosis and in a conscious state, were not enough, there were other reports describing the craft that night.

One couple reported that they saw a large and luminous round object near their home, which was several yards away from the abduction, around 11:30pm.

Two teenagers who were driving around claimed they chased the UFO all the way to Danville after it appeared over the Angel Manufacturing Plant in Stanford. Once they arrived in Danville, they reported what they saw to the local authorities.

The most convincing report came from the man who owned the property where the women said the abduction took place. He reported seeing a low-lying object shoot down a beam of light at the edge of his land.

Though many abduction reports have come through the pipes in the last several decades, many of which people scoff at, some that have been debunked, this one is very hard to contest. Given the thoroughness of the investigation, the consistency of the women's stories, the evidence on their bodies, and the number of eyewitnesses that can corroborate many parts of the account, one would have to be very obtuse to claim they were making it up. We believe it most definitely happened. The only part that is truly debatable is the nature of the abduction.

The strangest part of this case, we believe, lies in its historical documentation. Most other famous cases have been picked apart with skeptics offering derisive refutations against them. However, the Stanford case seems to have been swept under the rug. Is it because the testimonies are so ironclad, and the reputation of all three witnesses too credible to discount? There are no holes in their stories. Not only that, the physical evidence was upon their bodies. Debunking such a case seems next to impossible. Is that what keeps the story from being more notable? It could very well be that the story has been forgotten because these women never sought fame or money for their tale, which only solidifies its validity in our opinion. Regardless, the Stanford abduction is one of the most credible abduction cases ever reported.

THE CURIOUS DEATH OF THOMAS MANTELL

Though the Roswell Crash of 1947 remains the most popular UFO incident, Kentucky had its own mysterious aerial encounter with an unidentified craft not long after that event. In January of 1948, a twenty-five-year-old captain of the Kentucky Air National Guard, Thomas Mantell, found himself in pursuit of a UFO, a chase that began over Fort Knox and ended near Franklin.

On January 7th, an officer of the Kentucky Highway Patrol received reports out of Owensboro and Irvington about an unidentified craft roughly three-hundred feet in diameter heading west towards Godman Army Airfield at Ft. Knox. Around 1:45pm, several soldiers at Ft. Knox spotted the craft. They had described it as being mostly white, and roughly a third the size of a full moon. Those who observed the object from Clinton County Army Airfield (now known as Wilmington Air Park) in Ohio said it looked like a red cone wrapped in flames with a gaseous green mist trailing behind it. They observed it for more than a half hour. An eyewitness in Ohio's Lockbourne Army Airfield (now Rickenbacker Air National Guard Base) was able to see it in action. He said that it descended towards the ground, hovering low for about ten seconds before shooting back up into the sky. He estimated that it moved at a speed of 500mph when in level flight.

Thomas Mantell piloted one of the four F-51D Mustangs that were en route to approach the UFO. One of the planes was low on fuel, so that pilot had to return to base. As the remaining three planes approached, Mantell offered an up-close description of the craft. However, reports of this exchange have come up for dispute by those who actually heard it. This is allegedly the text from the transcript:

The object is directly ahead of and above me now, moving at about half my speed... It appears to be a metallic object or possibly reflection of sun from a metallic object, and it is of tremendous size... I'm still climbing... I'm trying to close in for a better look."

Mantell and the two remaining pilots continued their pursuit high into the sky. Command suggested that they level their altitudes in order to get a better view of the craft. Mantell ignored this suggestion and continued to follow the object higher. The other two pilots turned back at 22,500 feet. Mantell kept ascending until he flew too high and blacked out. The Mustang then began to spiral towards the earth and leveled off at about 30,000 feet before plummeting to the land below. The UFO disappeared from the area soon after, but sightings continued as it headed south towards Tennessee. When firefighters pulled the captain's destroyed body from the wreckage, they found that his watch had stopped at 3:18, which was the time of the crash.

As coverage of the event reached a national level and talks of aliens arose. The *New York Times* released an article titled, "Flier Dies Chasing a Flying Saucer." Another headline elsewhere read, "Plane Exploded over Kentucky as That and Near States Report Strange Object." This sparked many theories from experts in the extraterrestrial.

There were some claiming Mantell's plane had been shot down by an alien craft. The original Air Force research group that investigated UFO claims, Project Sign, stated that Mantell had actually been chasing the planet Venus. They drew this conclusion from a report that Venus had been the target of an F-51 chase a few weeks earlier. This report was later deemed incorrect due to the overcast in the sky that night. It is believed the pilots would not have been able to view Venus because of it. Had it been visible, it would have been nothing more than a pinpoint of light, and the pilots had described the object as a large illuminated ball.

Franklin resident and alleged eyewitness, Glen Mays, contested this theory as well, because of what he claimed to see. He stated that the plane began to fly in a circle, as if the pilot had no idea where he was going. Then it began a nosedive at about 20,000 feet. About halfway to the ground, the plane exploded. Also, Commander Guy F. Hix at Godman Air Field stated that he had observed the unidentified craft through binoculars for about an hour, and there was no possible way he would have mistaken that for Venus. To further wipe away this theory, astronomers insisted that Venus's placement in the sky at the time of the event would have made it impossible for the pilots to see, whether it was clear or overcast.

Another explanation was that Mantell had actually been chasing a Navy Skyhook weather balloon, which had allegedly been seen through a telescope by an observer in Madisonville. An astronomer at Vanderbilt University had spotted the object through binoculars at around 4:30pm and described it as a "pear-shaped balloon with cables and a basket attached". The Skyhooks were made of aluminum and about a hundred feet in diameter, which is somewhat consistent with the descriptions of the supposed UFO.

The Skyhooks were also classified technology at the time, so neither the pilots nor those in the tower would have known about their existence, which could be why they thought they were seeing a UFO. However, this explanation is sketchy because ever since the Skyhook project has been declassified, there are no records of this particular testing. The only bit of evidence is that someone working on the project "remembers" flying a balloon in that area. Thus, the report remains inconclusive.

There are some other points that UFOlogists believe contradicts this theory. One being that Richard T. Miller, who was present in the Operations Room at Scott Air Force Base in Belleville, IL, monitored the communications between Mantell and Godman and heard Mantell clearly say, "My God, I see people in this thing." He also stated that the following morning, investigators held a briefing and admitted that Mantell had "died chasing an intelligently controlled unidentified flying object." Later that evening, as Miller told it, Air Technical Intelligence Center officers demanded everyone turn over all material they had on the incident, and then declared that they had already completed the investigation.

To add to this suspicion, Capt. James F. Duesler, who was present at Godman when the event took place, admitted to having seen the craft. Soon after the crash, Duesler visited the site and gave some very telling and detailed reports of the aftermath. He stated that there was no real damage to the main body of the craft, and there was no blood in the cockpit. The propeller blade had little to no damage either, nothing to indicate that it had been spinning when the crash happened. The wings and tail looked to have broken off on impact and were lying very near to the plane, not scattered about, as they should have been if the reports were accurate. It appeared that the plane had just simply dropped without gliding or sliding along the ground, which was evident because none of the nearby trees had been damaged.

According to Duesler, a plane of this size with the weight of the nose and engine, would have hit the ground at an angle, damaging much of the frontend. Falling from that height, it would not have struck the ground and stayed in one spot, it would have most likely cut a swath through the trees, or at least bounced and scattered many of its parts. According to him, it was plain to see that there had been no forward or sideways mobility when the plan struck the ground. The condition of the plane and the reports made him suspicious.

To make the incident even more suspect, a cone-shaped craft was spotted flying over Clifton, North Carolina at incredible speeds the following day – January 8th. Also, on February 1st, residents of Circleville, Ohio reported a large metallic UFO shining a bright orange light onto the ground. There is no evidence that a Skyhook weather balloon is capable of emanating any light.

Mantell was an experienced and credible pilot, having flown in World War 2. In his career, he had earned an Air Medal with three Oak Leaf clusters, as well as the Distinguished Flying Cross for his courageous actions during Open Market Garden. His character was not in question regarding this incident. However, since there were rumors that his plane was shot down by the supposed alien craft, it has been pointed out that Mantell was inexperienced when it came to piloting the F-51. While this could have a bearing on why he crashed, it still does not explain the sighting.

It is unsure what Thomas Mantell died chasing that day. Though it is known that he was in pursuit of craft controlled by something intelligent, it has never been determined whether he was chasing a Skyhook weather balloon, or an alien UFO. Some remain skeptical, sure it was a weather balloon. Some don't know what to think, but keep an open mind. Others, however, are certain it was an alien craft. But even if the object of Mantell's pursuit remains unknown, what is known is that the Kentucky native was the first man to give his life chasing the UFO phenomenon.

*P5: Marker for Thomas Mantell, photo by Mark S. Hilton

THE KENTUCKY CROP CIRCLES

The crop circle phenomenon has been a staple of the alien encyclopedia ever since people began studying the concept of extraterrestrial life. Of course, no crop circles have ever proven aliens exist, and skeptics have long considered them elaborate hoaxes. But some of the reported crop circles have yielded some fascinating discoveries.

Crop circles are thought by some to be evidence of alien visitations – signs left by extraterrestrials, possibly as markers or ways to communicate with their kind. Skeptics have come forth with attempts to debunk these theories. Some have demonstrated how one can create their own crop circles. However, they are never able to leave designs as intricate as the mysterious patterns found by unsuspecting farmers and those flying overhead.

This enigmatic happening is no stranger to the farmlands and empty fields of the Bluegrass State. While Kentucky might not be at the center of the crop circle phenomenon, it certainly has a history of these astounding creations discovered from the sky.

In May of 2003, a large crop circle was observed in a Flemingsburg rye field along Tea Run Road. Jerry Wagner, sheriff of Fleming County, described it as perfectly round and fifty yards in diameter. There were several standing areas within the circle, including a mound of tall grass in the middle and some small bushes towards one of the edges. The circle appeared overnight, but was soon contaminated by flooding. Heavy storms hit the area and compromised the circle. But Wagner had seen it prior to the storms.

A few months later, in August, another crop circle was discovered about fifty miles away in a soybean field near the Serpent Mound State Memorial in Adams County, Ohio. This pattern was larger and much more elaborate than the one in Flemingsburg. It was about two-hundred feet in width and length, the design was intricate, with multiple circles, and it resembled some kind of ship. The night it formed, there were heavy storms and power outages in the area. An eyewitness reported seeing several balls of light that night flying around the formation's location. Upon investigation, the stalks were found flattened but their branches remained upright and unbroken. There was no sign of human entry into the circle.

The crop circle was approximately two-thousand feet from the mysterious Great Serpent Mound, which is an effigy mound located on a plateau of the Serpent Mound crater along Ohio Bush Creek. The mound is about three feet high, twenty-five feet wide, and 1,348 feet long. It is made of ash and yellowish clay reinforced with rocks and covered with soil. One of two prehistoric cultures is believed to have made the mound, either the Adena or the Fort Ancient.

The effigy is in the shape of a serpent whose body winds back and forth for about eight-hundred feet before ending in a triple-coiled tail. At the serpent's head, the mouth is open and extended around an oval-shaped figure believed to be either an egg or the sun. The purpose of the effigy has been up for debate for quite some time. Some believe it was a place for spiritual rituals, seeing as the serpent represents supernatural powers in cosmology and it matches the constellation, Draco. Others think it may have been inspired by astronomical events that occurred around 1070 AD, the year they believe it was created. Those events are the passing of Haley's Comet in 1066, or the supernova of 1054 that created the Crab Nebula. It might have been that the tribe that made this mound did so to commemorate said event. There is also a theory that the mound is a sort of compass. Whatever the mound represents, it seems the crop circle found near there was actually pointing toward the effigy.

The Serpent Mound in Ohio might be the most famous effigy mound but it is not the only one in existence. There are many across the United States, many of which contain evidence of burials. Most were created between 300 and 1300 CE. The age and number of these effigy mounds have sparked topics of aliens, and the Great Serpent Mound is widely believed to have alien connections.

Since many of these mounds were burial grounds for ancient civilizations, they have been excavated in hopes of learning more about the people who created them. Among the bones found were skeletons of what some believe are giants alleged to have roamed the Earth. Skeletons standing eight feet tall with thirty-six inch craniums have been removed from the mounds. Near the Great Serpent Mound in Ohio, a seven-foot skeleton was found.

Many believe these giants could have been extraterrestrials. This leads to theories about the Serpent Mound being an intergalactic portal, which explains why so many UFO sightings have occurred around it. It could also be why Ohio has more reported crop circles than any other state. That the mound lies within a five-mile crater created by an asteroid strike also raises questions. Is this snake effigy actually pointing to an opening in a bridge between Earth and another planet? Is that oval-shaped drawing in the serpent's mouth a craft, or a doorway? Perhaps the crop circle near the mound and the one in Flemingsburg are connected.

Flemingsburg is not the only Kentucky location where a crop circle has been discovered. There have been ten in all recorded in the last several decades. An eyewitness reported a circle of dead plants that had yellowed in Ashland in 1969. Also in Ashland, a different crop circle was reported near the Indian Mounds each year from 1985 until 1990. Another strange crop pattern appeared in Washington County in 1989. These reports were recorded but without much detail. But there was a more recent crop circle discovery that was much more peculiar.

On June 27th, 2004, a rancher discovered a very complex pattern in his field. The configuration was of a dozen circles, egg-shaped areas, and, coincidentally, several serpentine patterns weaving around the design. The manager contacted three friends to come to the ranch and see the designs; one of them was a woman suffering from skin cancer on her hand. The friends were quite surprised by what they saw.

The following day, the same four people visited the crop circles again. After spending roughly two hours in the field, they watched as another crop circle took shape. The people reported that their hands started to tingle and glow red, then sparks formed around their heads. Within one minute, the new circle had formed completely. The woman's skin cancer supposedly fell off her hand.

On June 29th, the owner found six more circles. This time, he decided that he was done with this unexplained development. He did not want media attention drawn to his ranch. So he mowed the grass through the entire field and eliminated the patterns.

All of these crop circles were in the northeastern section of Kentucky, nearer to southern Ohio. Ashland isn't much further from the Great Serpent Mound than Flemingsburg, and it had the most crop circles. Washington County is further to the southwest, but still lies on the eastern edge of central Kentucky. However, Versailles is less than an hour from Washington County, and it lies further to the east.

So while Ohio is the crop circle capital of the US, Kentucky might be picking up a lot of interstellar traffic from the possible space portal near the Great Serpent Mound. Not only were all the crop circles found in the eastern portion of the state, but most of Kentucky's alien activity leans towards the east. Not all of it, but enough to make you wonder.

Of course, it could all just be a major coincidence.

CATTLE KILLERS

Cattle mutilation is a most bizarre manner of killing livestock. In most cases, the animal is eviscerated and drained of blood. Eyes, ears, tongue, and rectum are often removed, as well. It happens mostly in North America, but has happened in other locations around the world. Many animals have been victim to this grisly affair, such as elk, deer, sheep, goats, and horses. But cattle are the most common.

Theories as to what may cause this macabre scene vary. Some think they are simply long-dead animals picked apart by scavengers and are in an advanced state of decay when discovered. Another theory is that these slayings are occult practices. There are those who point to cryptid animals attacking and feeding on the livestock. Then of course, there is the most popular fringe explanation: extraterrestrials.

Kentucky has had its share of cattle mutilations. But, before we get to that, let us talk about the history and possible meaning of this strange event.

Though this eerie phenomenon has been going on for centuries, the first real case to catch attention was in 1967 on the Harry King ranch near Alamosa, Colorado. A horse named Lady, that has since become known as Snippy, was found on her side with her skin stripped bare from the neck and shoulders, and her brain, lungs, digestive organs, and heart all removed with surgical precision. No traces of blood were found near or around the wounds. Some of the land around the horse was burned and there was an aroma of formaldehyde left at the scene. Two weeks later, the bones turned black.

Lady's owner, Nellie Lewis, reported that there had been exhaust marks and a flattened bush near the horse's body, and the area smelled of incense. When she picked up a piece of the horse's flesh, it burned her hand. A forestry official later detected a trace of radiation in the area. There were also six circular indentions, measuring about three feet in diameter, two inches across, and four deep, found around some nearby brush. There had also been UFO sightings reported in the area the night before Lady's corpse was found. A few weeks later, more horses and cattle were left in the same condition across ranches in the area. Many locals were convinced aliens were involved.

A few years later, a rash of cattle mutilations began in 1970 and continued through the ensuing decades. The FBI was asked to investigate, but were unable to in many cases as the mutilations did not occur in their jurisdiction. The only time they were involved was when the mutilations took place on Native American land. But, the animals were left in the same condition Lady had been, with the same nearly flawless surgical accuracy.

A 1995 report stated that about 8000 cattle and horses were mutilated in the aforementioned fashions. The attacks spread over eighteen states through the West, Midwest, and South, covering more than a million square miles, which constitutes more than a third of the country's landmass. To make matters more baffling, many of these mutilations were accompanied by UFO sightings. Once the investigation commenced, some strange evidence emerged.

As with Lady, many of the organs were removed from the corpses. All the blood had been carefully drawn from the bodies via small puncture holes in the jugular. Again, it looked as if expert hands had completed the work, as there were no visible signs of what had caused the animals' deaths and no traces of blood on or around the bodies.

No tire marks, footprints, or other signs of human presence were visible around the mutilations. In many of the cases, there were even no prints from the animals themselves. Many of the animals were found with their legs broken or their backs pushed into the ground, as if they were dropped from the sky.

The same trace elements were found on many of the bodies, ranging all throughout the affected area, which indicates the same forces were behind the entire rash of mutilations. Perhaps the oddest detail of all was that neither buzzards nor coyotes would feed on the carcasses. Perhaps this could have something to do with the trace elements.

In 2001, a two-month-old Appaloosa colt belonging to Mike and Rose Downs was found dead in a pasture in Leitchfield with a one-inch hole in its chest. Grayson County Sheriff Joe Brad Hudson said he found no exit wounds, no shells or casings, and no blood around the animal. The colt's reproductive organs were gone.

A year before that, a neighbor to the Downses, Leonard Bruner, found one of his heifer calves in similar condition just outside the woods on the outskirts of his farm. Like the colt, the calf was missing its reproductive organs, and there was no blood on the body or the ground around it. The tongue and one ear had been removed.

A few years prior to that, a man named Moran Mudd, who lived about ten miles to the south in a town called Sadler, found one of his Hereford bull's had suffered the same dismemberment. The bull was found in a small streambed on Mudd's farm with its sexual organs removed, no blood and no bullet holes. The hooves had been so cleanly separated from the feet that Mudd thought they had fallen off. They were later found on a flat rock nearby, lined up just as they were on the bull's feet. Hair from the bull's tail was hanging from a tree branch about four feet off the ground. Mudd also claimed that the buzzards wouldn't touch the animal.

Such mutilations have been occurring around Grayson County since 1976. In all that time, there have been no arrests and no conclusive explanations as to what or who is responsible. Police have considered the possibility of cult activity, but have never been able to find any evidence to validate this suspicion.

As you can see, the Leitchfield incidents are very similar to those reported throughout the United States in the 70s. The Leitchfield area was a part of that rash of mutilations and it seems that it continued for decades. The curious nature of these kills has led people to believe extraterrestrials are responsible. Many feel it could be a method of studying the creatures on this planet. To those who believe, it is a logical deduction considering they are allegedly abducting humans, as well. It makes sense that they would possibly want to study the animal life on Earth, too.

It could also have something to do with the random meat showers that were discussed earlier in this book. Perhaps in the 1800s, the alien visitors weren't as familiar with the livestock, and so they took the entire bodies up into their crafts, studied them, took what they needed, and discarded the remains. We reiterate, maybe they devised a new method, and decided to come down to Earth and do the studies here, take what they needed, and leave the remains where they lay. Skeptics of course would find this preposterous, but believers would not.

Now, an alternate explanation to cattle mutilation sounds just as cloak-and-dagger even if it's more "down to Earth". It has been thought that maybe there is a secret organization going around monitoring the food chain to prevent an outbreak of bovine spongiform, or Mad Cow Disease.

Of course, many animal experts believe that the mutilations are simply the work of predators. They say such animals can do some very thorough work on their prey. However, there are no animals known for guzzling eleven pounds of blood and leaving a dried-up carcass behind otherwise intact. Limbs would be chewed, bones broken, and the entry points would not be so exact. Most believe this is likely not the work of predatory animals.

So who was it? Was it the secret food chain monitoring organization? Was it cryptids? Was it aliens? These answers are still out there.

THE UNEXPLAINABLE CYLINDER

Among the thousands of UFOs reported in history, there are a few common varieties. The most famous is the flying saucer, or discus-shaped craft, which has been seen for decades. There have also been triangular, spherical, and cylindrical (cigar-shaped) UFOs reported and videotaped, as well. Cylinder crafts are reported quite often.

On August 4th, 2016, a woman and man in New York were driving home between nine and 10pm when they spotted a strange light in the sky. They watched it for a few seconds and were shocked to see they were looking at a silver cylinder-shaped craft. They recorded it for a few minutes and uploaded it to YouTube.

In March of 2017, a family in Australia witnessed a cylinder UFO flying at about five-hundred feet. The child pointed up to the sky and said, "Moon." The parents looked up and saw the craft moving quickly through the sky. The woman suggested the man record it, so he did. The video is inconclusive and hard to discern anything more than a small shape flying through the air. MUFON has documented the incident.

These are just two examples. There are websites dedicated to tracking UFO reports, and there are databases specifically for the cylinder ship. Reports have been coming in for the last twenty years regarding this style of UFO, and some even further back, in the 80s, 60s, and even the 30s. Some explanations claim these objects to be balloons of some kind, and others have said the cylinder is nothing more than a blimp. But many believe them to be alien airships.

Kentucky's had a few cylinders floating in its skies over the years. Many of the reports are vague and come from anonymous sources. Naturally, these cases were not investigated and remain inconclusive. However, there are others that seem more legitimate.

One of these crafts was allegedly spotted near Ft. Knox in 1967. Two people in their backyard saw a glowing, bright, silver cylindrical object land on a hillside near their home. They decided to approach the craft and investigate. When they got within a hundred yards, the cylinder ascended into the sky and flew away. No confirmation ever came from any sources outside the report, so it may have been a hoax.

In July of 1984, an eyewitness who saw the cylinder craft floating in the sky over Irvington decided to call the county sheriff. The sheriff then informed him that several people across the county had been calling in and reporting the same unidentified object that evening. Several residents of neighboring Meade County reported seeing this UFO, as well.

An eyewitness report came from an alleged ex-paratrooper in Owensboro regarding an alleged sighting in 1986. The witness states they were driving north on a clear, cloudless day and had to stop at a traffic light. As they waited for the light to change, they looked up into the sky and saw something spiraling towards the earth. Curious to see what this object was, the witness crossed the intersection when the light turned green and pulled into the parking lot of an abandoned building and got out to watch the event. They determined what they saw was a metallic object, shaped like a cylinder with two spherical apertures on each side, flipping end over end, scooting a little between each flip. Each movement was seamless and quick, and the airship was capable of motions no known human plane or aircraft were. The witness also reports that two jets were trailing the object at an altitude of no less than 2000 feet, and were aligned in a half-V formation. The craft they were chasing did not appear to have lights or openings, and seemed to be smooth and without creases. The witness continued to observe this graceful aircraft until it disappeared to the south. Once gone, the witness looked to see if anyone else had been watching, but no one else took notice. After arriving home, they contacted the local air traffic control center to inquire about the ship. ATC had not seen it and had received no reports.

A very interesting report came out of Lexington in 2002. A family and a few friends were in their backyard by Man o' War Boulevard on a summer morning, between three and 5am. They heard a jet flying overhead, with the engine whining as if strained. They believed the plane to be in some sort of distress. They soon noticed a cylindrical object flying in front of it. It was much larger than the plane, and as they watched, it stopped, opened a compartment in its hull, and the struggling jet vanished inside. The giant cylinder then sped off in a streak of bright light, causing an explosion in the early morning sky. After pondering the event, they went to sleep, and they say they awoke the next day with no memory of it. It wasn't until someone mentioned a UFO a few years later that the recollection returned.

Also in 2002, a man in Hopkinsville saw two jets pursued by a large, cylinder craft that had no wings attached to it. At first, he saw only the two jets. A few seconds later, he saw what he said looked like a star in the sky near them, but the "star" soon disappeared. The jets then veered right and the observer looked up and saw that the large, silver, cylindrical ship was now in the sky above him. Unlike the jets, it left no vapor trails. The jets then turned once again and were now the ones in pursuit. He was later shown some photographs of a cylinder-shaped UFO and determined it was very much like what he saw in the sky that day.

In February 2004, a Cessna pilot flying over Blackey said he spotted a cylinder-shaped aircraft to his left at about 2:45am. The pilot was only about two minutes outside of Hazard Airport, so he gave them a call to see if they could identify it, they could not. He claims to have gotten four snapshots of the object. However, these photos have not been made public and the pilot wished to remain anonymous. The validity of this report is questionable.

Someone in Smithland saw this type of craft in 2006 hovering in the air as they drove a few miles east of town. The driver rolled down the window to watch the object. It was large, cylindrical, and metallic, and it left no trails in the sky. A few minutes later, the driver pulled onto the shoulder to avoid traffic and watch the craft. By the time they were parked and looking back to the sky, the craft was gone.

A couple in Lancaster claim to have caught a UFO on a deer camera in 2011. The camera was placed in an open field with no lights, roads, or homes in the vicinity. Eventually, they say a long, cylinder-shaped craft with bright lights appear. They said they could tell it was not a train or an airplane, but a craft that stayed visible for several minutes. We could not find a picture of this, but it made us think of the trail camera incident in Biloxi, MS where a couple caught a pair of lights in the sky over a deer's head. They thought this was a UFO but the two lights were actually the reflection of the deer's eyes bouncing around inside the infrared lens.

The cylinder returned to Owensboro in 2012. It was seen flying quickly over the city, heading southeast. It was described as shiny and soundless.

Later that same year, the craft was seen hovering over a Kroger's in the Fern Creek neighborhood of Louisville. It was very bright and accompanied by two other objects that were harder to define. All three hovered in the air for quite some time over Seatonville Road before disappearing. This was the second report of UFOs in this area.

Still in 2012, a family in Belfry watched the cylinder in the sky for nearly an hour. They were heading down Highway 119 when their daughter asked, "What's that in the sky?" They looked up and saw the large, mirrored object floating along. They said it moved like a bird, swooping and turning gracefully. They pulled over to watch it. Slowly, it rose into the sky until it was out of sight. A little while later, the daughter said, "There it is again." They rode home and saw their neighbor watching the sky with a pair of binoculars. They asked if he was watching the craft too, which he was. They all watched it for a few minutes until it was gone.

Five reports of a cylinder moving through the sky were issued out of Pikeville in October of 2012. Some even took video, which revealed a bright cylinder hanging in the sky. Most believed this to be yet another UFO. However, an amateur astronomer by the name of Allan Epling says that it was just a very bright daylight star. He points out that you can see in the video that the shape is not moving. Though the cylinder has been reported to hover, this still could explain the phenomenon. Perhaps many of the reports about cylindrical UFOs have been a result of the same daylight star.

A cylinder with bright lights shining out from it and red lights on top was spotted in 2013 over a neighborhood in Erlanger. An eyewitness was out smoking on their balcony when they saw it hover over the neighborhood. They watched it for a few minutes until it ascended into the thick clouds and disappeared.

In 2016, a woman was driving through Lexington at about 10pm when she saw a bright light in the sky to her left. She thought nothing of it, assuming it was a star, until she noticed it was getting closer. She then decided it was a helicopter because of how low it was coming in. As it passed over top of her, she was shocked at what she saw. The craft looked like a missile or spaceship, cylinder in shape and without wings, with a bright blue light shining from the bottom. She was certain this was no helicopter or commercial airliner.

Whatever this cylinder-shaped object is, witnesses have seen it many times over Kentucky. Of course, some of the reports above could have easily been hoaxes or sightings of some military craft. But, if true, all the reports seem to offer very similar details. If it really were capable of allowing jets to dock inside of it while still in the air, that makes it impossible that it would be a blimp or balloon. Has it been the same craft all these years? If so, why is it here? Guess for now, we'll just have to make do with speculation and supposition.

BLACK TRIANGLES

One of the most common UFO crafts is the black triangle. These shadowy ships are usually low-lying, silent, witnessed at night, and have pulsing lights along their underbellies, aligned in a triangle. Initially, reports of these black triangles came out of the United States and the United Kingdom. They have been spotted by eyewitnesses and have appeared on radar.

Among the most noted cases of black triangle sightings occurred in Belgium from November 1989 to April 1990. For several months, witnesses spotted these UFOs across the country, with the most curious incident happening in March when a pair of Belgium Air Force F-16s investigated an unidentified craft appearing on radar. Neither pilot ever saw the craft. During this time, eyewitnesses on the ground claimed to have seen the triangles flying in the area. After this, reports of the ships continued for weeks. This became known as the Belgium UFO Wave.

Another well known incent happened in Phoenix, AZ in 1997. Several of the crafts and unidentified lights were videotaped and photographed for several days, beginning on March 13th. Some of these lights were seen moving too slowly to be jets, too silently to be helicopters, and at levels as low as 1000 feet. Some witnesses reported a black triangle flying over their houses and blocking out the stars, estimating the ship to be over a mile wide. The military eventually issued a statement claiming they had been testing flares shot from military craft during that time, and that was what people had seen. However, some eyewitnesses maintain that while there were indeed jets flying out of nearby Luke Air Force Base, they weren't shooting off flares, they were pursuing the black triangles. This incident is known as the Phoenix Lights.

These are just two of the most documented black triangle cases. Many more have occurred through the years. Kentucky has had its share of black triangle UFOs, as well. There are many reports to be found, but some are very vague. We combed through dozens and included some of the more detailed accounts in this chapter.

A man from Texas reported an incident he had back when he was a boy living in Kirksey, Kentucky in 1963. He said that he remembered walking out into the garden at his home, with his dog walking by his side, when he stopped at the gate and, for some unknown reason, looked back over his shoulder. When he did, he was frightened to see a triangular silver craft hovering silently in the sky not too far away. The craft appeared to have a nose and the boy could see a pilot inside. It scared him so much than he ran back to the house screaming for his mother. When he got her to come outside, he looked to the sky and the craft had vanished. He never told anyone but close friends and relatives of this incident until 2008.

A man was returning home from visiting his wife in Lourdes Hospital in Smithland in 1975 when he saw five amber lights floating along the sky in a triangular formation. At first, he could not tell if these lights emanated from one object or five. So he stopped his car to get out and observe. Upon doing so, he could see the lights were connected to one triangular-shaped object about a quarter-mile wide. The object was moving quietly from east to west, and on a steady glide. The man returned to his car to continue following the object. He eventually found himself on Court Street, which brought him to a dead end near the Cumberland River. It was there he stopped his car again to watch the object disappear behind an expanse of woods running along the Illinois shoreline. He later found out that similar objects had been reported along the East Coast around the same time, but none in his immediate area.

A group of campers at Land Between the Lakes in 1982 noticed some strange lights over the lake around 11pm. From atop a ridge, they looked down and saw that the lights came from a craft about six-hundred yards across, black, silent, triangular, and had lights running the color spectrum at each corner. It ran about two-hundred feet on each side with a ten-foot-high raised pyramid in the center. They saw a blue light inside the craft through the ports that were on top of it, and movement could be detected in the foreground of that light. A light would shine intermittently from the bottom of the craft to the ground. The object hovered about forty minutes, emitting only a low humming sound from time to time, before slowly rising into the sky. The campers watched in awe as the craft began to pick up speed and eventually vanish quickly into the night.

A man in Yelvington in 1984 spotted a roaring triangle about the size of three football fields in length hovering in the sky less than a mile above his home. Lights that kept changing colors surrounded the massive ship. Soon, three smaller crafts emerged from the bottom of it. The witness claimed to have served in the military and could not identify these strange crafts.

In 1986, an amateur astronomer in Tompkinsville was observing the passing of Haley's Comet when he saw a giant L-shaped triangle ship fly silently into view. He watched it pass slowly overhead and saw that the bottom was flat but with I-beam and circular structures underneath and no lights. It was as big as an airliner and had a dull, metallic look to it. He thought it resembled a larger Stealth bomber, only slow and silent.

Also in 1986, a man was at his home in Hazard when he saw a spotlight shining down from an object in the sky about a half-mile away, having just flown in over a mountaintop. For a moment, the light shined on him. It was so bright all he could see was the light. He thought it could have been a helicopter, but he noticed it made no sound. He went into his house to get his wife and father-in-law. By the time they had gotten out into the street, the craft had risen into the air. They could then see the craft was shaped like an isosceles triangle with lights on each tip. As it passed overhead, they judged that it was rather large. It glided past them silently and disappeared over the next mountain.

In 1991, a man was driving north in Crittenden along 1-75 when his truck broke down. After working on it for a while to no avail, he began walking towards the next exit. After passing under an overpass, he emerged to a bright light shining down on him. This startled him at first because he hadn't heard anything in the sky, and there was no traffic in either direction. He assumed that someone was up on the overpass shining a spotlight upon him. Not wanting to remain in the light, the man stepped back under the overpass. When he stepped back out, the light was gone, and he saw a triangle craft in the moonlight, suspended about two-hundred feet above the overpass. It appeared to be about a hundred feet in length and cast no reflection of the starlight. As with most other reports, the ship was silent, and rose slowly into the air at first, before ascending rapidly and disappearing.

A family was travelling to Alabama in 1994 and stopped in Louisville for a break. After everyone had gone to the restroom and stretched, the family got back in the car and continued driving south on the interstate. Soon, they noticed a lighted object in the sky. The father joked that it was a UFO, but he wouldn't be laughing for long. The object rushed at them until it was flying above their car. The craft was a black, silent, triangle about the size of a football field, and it was just a few stories over top of them. Three lights shone down on them as they drove along in fear of this menacing machine. After following them for a few minutes, the craft began to ascend, then took off away from them and disappeared. However, to make the incident more curious, when the object first appeared it was 11pm, when it departed, it was 2:30am, and to the family, the incident only felt like a few minutes. Could this also be a case of abduction?

A young man returning from playing *Dungeons and Dragons* at a comic book store he owned in Elizabethtown in 1995 looked up and saw a black craft much larger than a football field above him. He was not able to discern the shape at first since it was nighttime, but due to the orange and red lights pulsing at each corner, he could make out the silhouette of a triangle. The craft hovered over him as he drove along. It made no noise the entire way. Two police officers also spotted the craft from Ring Road. An article was allegedly written about this incident in the local paper, *The News Enterprise*, and it stated that the government would investigate the sightings. After doing so, their conclusion was that the lights were reflections from the fireworks show at the Heartland Festival. The witness is sure that this was no firework reflection, as he drove beneath this craft for some time.

In April of 2002, a family in Ewing was nearing their home and saw some lights in the sky near their house. At first, they thought maybe a helicopter was in the area, possibly hunting down a fugitive. But when they got home, they saw a black triangle with a light at each corner hovering over the end of their driveway, just high enough to clear the trees. It was silent and moved very slowly until it was gone from sight.

In 2007, a YouTuber by the name of Tom Levine uploaded a video titled, *Black Triangle Kentucky 2-22-07 Sighting*. It doesn't state where at in Kentucky this video was recorded, but it shows some very mysterious lights hovering in the blackened sky in the distance. Some comments on the video claim the lights are from a blimp. However, this is unverified.

There were a couple of sightings in 2009. The first was in Stanton on March 18th, over Mountain Parkway. The witness was driving to work and saw the large, black craft in the sky ahead of him. The lights on the front of the craft caught his attention, and he noticed it was hovering over the nearby trees. At first, he thought it was a plane or helicopter, but as he drew closer, he could see the ship's triangular form. He said the object made no sound. Disturbed by this sighting, he sped past the object. When he looked in his rearview mirror, the ship was no longer in sight.

The other sighting happened in Louisville on March 30th. A man described seeing a triangle-shaped craft with a dent in its center and a row of lights running from tip to end, a red light bringing up the rear, hovering in the sky as he was driving. He slowed down to try and get a picture of it and could see that it was dark gray at the top and light gray at the bottom. The craft then disappeared behind a tree line, only to come back into view travelling slowly, just a few feet above a row of houses. The man then turned down a side street and saw a second similar object fly by in the distance for about a minute. After doubling back around to the side street, he found another triangle hovering silently over his vehicle. It took off suddenly when he was close to his house. He parked in front of his home and watched as three triangles flew away.

Someone smoking a cigarette outside their mother-in-law's home in Chaplin, Kentucky claimed to have spotted two triangles about 150 yards above the ground. Upon seeing the first craft, they thought nothing of it because it moved so slowly. They figured it was military. It had a green-orange light in each corner, and it was quite noisy, setting it apart from many of the other reports regarding the black triangles. The witness went back inside and not soon after, heard the same rumbling jet sound they'd heard before. They returned outside and saw another triangle craft, only this time they were quite shocked at what they saw. In the center of the ship was a spinning neon blue orb. This alarmed them and they returned inside the house.

On July 15th, 2014, a couple was in their backyard in Lexington when a black triangle suddenly began hovering over their house. The woman noticed it first and watched it for a second before pointing it out to her boyfriend. Together, they determined it was definitely dark and triangular. She thinks it was pointing east, and as they both continued to watch it, they say it begin to rotate as if it was on an axis, and point west. Then, it suddenly took off without sound, vanishing quickly from sight, leaving behind no vapor trail.

In 2016, a young man in Louisville claimed to have been looking at his phone and found Google Maps open for some unknown reason. When he looked at the image on the screen, he saw a black triangle hovering in the clouds over his home. He showed it to his father, who then reported it to MUFON (case 81433).

A veteran UFO hunter by the name of Scott Waring was convinced that the father and son had spotted an actual UFO. Waring found the coordinates, screenshot the images, and posted them to his blog, *UFO Sightings Daily*. He concluded that the triangle was in fact there above the house, but that was not all. As he navigated Google Maps down the road a ways, he could see that the triangle remained, and appeared to be following the Google Maps car. In one picture, it was in front of the trees, so Waring deduced that the craft must be no larger than one meter from corner to corner, and that it was possibly using a cloaking device, but the camera's digital eye caught it anyway. He went on to mention how Google has a tool that blurs faces and license plates, and claimed that they must be blurring UFOs now, too. He noted that the blur on the UFO was the same as the blur across the home's windows. The pictures are quite interesting, though it looks like it could possibly be something on the camera lens, but perhaps not. When we checked the listed coordinates, we found that the Google images have been changed.

These are only some of the accounts of the black triangle in Kentucky. Most of the other reports are very similar. Someone travelling alone or standing outside of their house sees the craft, describes it roughly the same, and then has the same experience of it ascending quickly out of sight.

In this case, the Frightening Floyds have our own experience to add. We were driving down Preston Highway in the Hillview-Okolona area, which is a southern section of Louisville, one evening in 2018 when we saw a triangular-shaped craft hovering by an electrical tower near Burger King. What initially caught our attention were the lights. There was one light at each corner, changing from white to red. The sky still held a hint of evening blue, and the lights shining from the numerous stores and businesses in Hillview provided enough illumination to see that the object was clearly dark and triangular. Shocked by what we were seeing, we pulled over onto the highway's grassy median to observe the craft. We watched as it hovered there for a few seconds. We rolled down our windows and could hear no sound. Suddenly, it began to tilt vertically, pointing its nose into the air. It stayed in that position for a few seconds before leveling out again. We then decided to get our camera and take a picture. By the time we had the camera out and ready, the craft had vanished. What it was, we cannot say.

This area is very near to Louisville International Airport, which shares land with the world's largest UPS hub. Planes are constantly in the sky, day and night, so we are used to seeing regular planes, jets, and airliners soaring overhead, as we have been seeing them all our lives. This did not look anything like those. It was at a very low altitude and was definitely not a UPS plane or any kind of commercial airliner. Furthermore, it was not heading towards the airport, nor was it heading away. It was stationary, and we don't know where it went when it vanished.

We do not rule out the possibility that this was a military craft. Many triangle UFO sightings have been attributed to the TR-B3 military craft, which is a triangular-shaped plane. We are also about thirty-five miles from Fort Knox. Whenever they test weapons there, we can hear them firing. So, it's quite possible what we saw was a military plane. Why it would have been hovering near a virtually inconsequential electrical tower in the middle of a densely populated small town such as Hillview is hard to tell. We don't have those answers; we just know what we saw. The rest, as with all the other black triangle tales, is speculation.

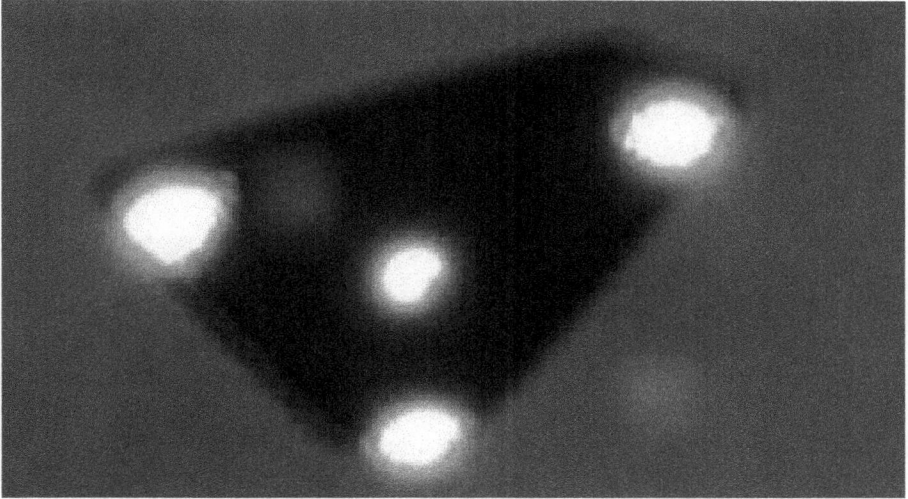

*P6: Black Triangle, courtesy of J.S. Henrardi

THE KENTUCKY MOTHMAN

Thanks to the chilling 2002 film *The Mothman Prophecies*, based on the book of the same name by John Keel, most people have heard of the mysterious Mothman of Point Pleasant, West Virginia. He was believed to have been a harbinger of doom, whose arrival preceded the tragic Silver Bridge collapse that killed forty-six people on December 15th, 1967. Before the collapse, many townsfolk had reported seeing him, as well as strange men in black, around town. Author John Keel investigated the claims while they were transpiring, and chronicled his findings in his book.

While many believe the sightings to be a hoax, the legend of the Mothman has endured in the paranormal community. Some believe he was some sort of supernatural manifestation; others believe he is a cryptid; most insist he was extraterrestrial. It's not surprising some would believe this, considering the frequent sightings and even confrontations with mysterious men in black in Point Pleasant while the sightings were taking place.

However, the Point Pleasant event may be the Mothman's most notorious account; it is not a lone occurrence. In 1938, residents around the Kentucky towns of Ashland and Elizabethtown, cities a little more than two-hundred miles apart, reported seeing a large, black humanoid creature with bright red eyes and a giant wingspan. Many residents reported the creature flying through town, perched in trees and on top of buildings. The sighting stopped abruptly in 1939. Since the Mothman has come to be known as a herald of catastrophe, many have speculated as to what his purpose in Kentucky could have been. Some people think it was the coming war in Europe. But what does that have to do with Kentucky? Being that he was spotted in Ashland brings us back to the possible portal not far from there in Ohio. Maybe he was just passing through.

In 2003, someone captured photos of the alleged Mothman on top of a river bridge in Russell, which is a stone's throw from Ashland. There are two photos. One shows the "creature" perched atop the bridge, and it appears to be black with glowing eyes, though the glow could have simply been a result of lightening the picture. The second image shows whatever it is falling, leaping, or flying off the bridge. The pictures are grainy and inconclusive, but interesting nonetheless. No tragedies took place in Russell after that, so who knows why the Mothman would have been there.

In 2008, the Mothman returned to either Elizabethtown or Ashland (the report doesn't state which; it just comes with the 1938 report). Farmer Harley Foster said he saw the Mothman perched atop his barn. He described the creature as bird-like with bright red eyes. Once he noticed the Mothman, it flew after him. Foster ran and was chased for a while before finally escaping the frightening form. No catastrophes occurred in the area afterwards.

It's possible that the Mothman isn't a bringer of bad tidings. The incident in Point Pleasant may have been coincidental. A mysterious being named Indrid Cold predicted the bridge collapse, not the Mothman. There were also men in black wandering about the town. It seems like the Point Pleasant Mothman case had outside forces. Maybe this Mothman, whatever it is, is just a large bird often mistaken for something else. Maybe it's cryptid or alien. West Virginia isn't far from Kentucky, especially Ashland and Russell, which border West Virginia as well as Ohio, which we've already established as having great extraterrestrial significance; perhaps it is connected to the many unexplained happenings taking place in our state.

At the Mothman Museum in Pt. Pleasant, WV. Was he here in Kentucky, too?

EXTRATERRESTRIAL EASTERN KENTUCKY

We already speculated in the crop circle chapter about how the eastern side of the state may receive more alien activity because of its close proximity to Ohio's Great Serpent Mound, which some believe could be an intergalactic portal. We must reiterate that we are not claiming to take a stance on this matter, but are merely reporting the theory and possibility. Despite what one's position might be on the matter, the truth is that eastern Kentucky receives an abundance of reported extraterrestrial experiences.

According to MUFON's Kentucky director, David MacDonald, who is also assistant director of investigations for the volunteer agency dedicated to investigating and documenting UFO reports, the area along the Big Sandy River (which coincidentally runs north along the border of Kentucky and West Virginia and ends at Ohio) and down into Bowling Green, has been a real hotbed of reports. Being a commercial airline pilot gives MacDonald some aerial insight, and in 2011, he discussed some incidents in the neighboring counties of Greenup, Boyd, and Carter.

On February 11th, a couple who had been delivering papers for Greenup-based newspaper *The Independent* for about seven years were on their route when they had an unexpected encounter with an unidentified craft. As they were driving along, they noticed police officers parked in a local animal clinic gazing at the dark morning sky with binoculars. When the couple asked them what they were looking at, the officers told them they received a call about a UFO. The call came in around 2:30am and described a UFO with a pulsing red light darting around in the sky. The officer handed the binoculars to the husband so he could look for himself. When he looked through the binoculars, the husband saw an oblong, cigar-shaped craft with red and green lights hovering in the sky. He claimed to have watched the craft for about ten minutes. The wife described the object as being too high to be a helicopter but not high enough to be an airplane. It then rose quickly into the sky and vanished to the west. Neither the couple nor the officers had any idea what the craft could have been. The husband had served in the military and said he knew it was no helicopter. An employee of the Ashland Regional Airport in Worthington confirmed the airport had been closed that night and was unaware of any aircraft in the sky at those hours. Air traffic control also had no indications of any planes or crafts in the sky around the time.

Also in 2011, a woman walking her dog through the Green Hills Subdivision in Ashland around 3am looked up and noticed what she thought was a bright star suddenly appear in the sky. She commented to her dog about the size of it, and then noticed the star was getting closer. Soon, it was upon her. She then noticed it was not a star, but a cigar-shaped craft hovering in the clear winter sky. It stayed for only a minute or so before rising quickly and vanishing out of sight.

In Cannonsburg, which borders Ohio, a woman named Rachel was driving her husband to work when her son noticed something bright, like flashes of lightning, in the darkened sky. She advised him to take pictures of it with his iPhone, so he did. After looking them over, he told Rachel that he caught something strange in the photographs, and that he thought it was a UFO. His mother agreed that it was quite odd after looking at it, but said she wouldn't be surprised if it was just a smudge on the lens.

An anonymous poster from an area near the border of West Virginia shared a rather bizarre experience they had in February of 2016. This person claimed that someone approached them on the 16th and told them that they would see something strange that night. They say that night they saw a craft come out of the sky and fly low to the ground, then move quickly across the sky. They claim that in 2015, they witnessed four UFOs make a wormhole in the sky that an alien mother ship came through. They went on to say they believe they have been led on a path by someone to learn secrets about ancient aliens, and that they believed someone was monitoring them in hopes of preventing them from pursuing that course.

For many years, there were reports of pulsing red and green lights in the sky over eastern Kentucky, specifically in the Greenup area.

In June of 2015, a slow-moving, chevron-shaped craft with a constantly glowing light appeared in the Greenup sky for about five minutes. During this time, a second craft appeared, flew near to the first, and then disappeared. The main craft did not behave like a fighter jet, airliner, helicopter, balloon, satellite, or shooting star. It had a very odd pattern of movement and almost looked to be moving sideways. The lights were not consistent with that of a normal plane or satellite.

On February 19th, 2017, two witnesses standing on a ridge near Greenup's industrial parkway saw three objects glowing an off-green color come into view in the sky. One object landed on the ground while the others continued to hover. Their lights dissipated like heat and then they vanished. They made whirring and clapping sounds as they moved, but disappeared in a thunderous bang. The object that sat on the ground below the onlookers remained, so they decided to take a picture of it. When they turned on their phones, there was a strange interruption in the devices, like static. The object suddenly rose into the air and vanished with a loud boom. The witnesses left immediately after and had to pull over on the freeway because of a severe onset of nausea. Both became very ill after this incident.

In 2018, a witness reported seeing randomly flashing lights in the sky move at varying speeds from north to south. They would flash slowly, pulsing a bright silver, and then dim out. The lights seemed to hover at some points and then slightly change directions until eventually they were heading east instead of south. The lights became dimmer before slowly disappearing altogether. This was the second night the witness had observed such activity. Due to the close proximity of a couple of local airports, the witness may have simply seen an average airplane in flight, though this has not been verified. But, because of all the unexplained sightings in that area through the years, it's worth some consideration.

Sightings over eastern Kentucky aren't just recent, either. Boone County, on the northern border of the eastern half of the state, close to Ohio, had some reports of strange crafts in the sky back in 1955. On May 31st, several witnesses in Burlington reported seeing a group of metallic objects that were flat, round, and broad with a V-shape towards their tail ends flying over town in the daylight hours. The objects were very bright and shiny, and they flew in formation.

As in previous chapters, these are but a few of the unexplained sightings in eastern Kentucky. We've already discussed our possible theory. As you can see, the areas with the majority of incidents are not far from Ohio. Are these alien sightings or just military testing their crafts far from the major cities?

MYSTERY BLIPS

On December 10th, 2018, a line of mysterious blips that came across the radar over southern Illinois and western Kentucky baffled the National Weather Service. The technical anomaly appeared to be a line of storms moving across the area, but there were no storms taking place – no wind, no rain, no lightning, and no thunder. The sky was clear, yet these blips floated across the screen.

The following day, after much speculation, Eyewitness News meteorologist Wayne Hart claimed that an unnamed Evansville pilot reported that a C-130 had released chaff in the air a few miles northwest of Evansville, Indiana. Chaff is a radar-jamming substance military aircraft sometimes use during training exercises. At first, this explanation made sense considering there are two military bases near the area: Fort Campbell in Kentucky and Scott Air Force Base in western Illinois.

However, it turns out that if a C-130 did in fact release chaff into the air, it did not come from either of those bases. A master sergeant from Scott Air Force Base insisted that the plane definitely did not come from their location while a spokesperson from Fort Campbell stated if the aircraft came from their installation, he was not aware of it.

Further investigation into the matter saw the story quickly change. The plane that released the chaff was allegedly a C-130H Hercules from the West Virginia Air National Guard on its way back to Charleston after a training exercise at an unnamed location on the west coast. According to sources from the base, the plane needed to release the excess chaff as a safety precaution before it landed. The pilot had received permission to do so from Indianapolis Center.

This explanation seems sketchy to many. The anonymous nature of this supposed training exercise and the unknown west coast location it took place at raise questions. The amount of chaff released from the plane would have to have been quite substantial, and weather conditions just right, for it to not only cause such a massive blip, but to also have it last for more than ten hours while travelling across two states. The Federal Aviations Commission has regulations when it comes to dumping chaff because they do not want potentially dangerous disruptions in air traffic. Also, it was determined that the chaff was released at 10,000 feet, which is well below the C-130's cruising altitude, and this is quite an odd practice. Not to mention how strange it was that the pilot would wait 2000 miles before dropping the chaff, since there were many other locations between the west coast and Kentuckiana to have done so. The explanation doesn't add up in the eyes of many people.

Even if this explanation is accurate, it doesn't account for the radar blips that occurred in Maine and Florida around the same time. On December 12th, blips popped up on a Portland, Maine radar as well as on radar over the Florida Keys. While it could be that military exercises were taking place, especially around Florida where they are common, there is only one military base near Portland and it is believed no planes there carry chaff. Furthermore, here is no confirmation that any military exercises were taking place near either of those locations.

There are other theories about this blip besides chaff. Some said a large flock of birds might have caused it, but that is not likely. If birds could do that, it would no doubt occur a lot more often, and an avian flock that large would not go unnoticed. Others thought bits of a passing asteroid had gotten into our atmosphere and showed up on radar, but there was no asteroid detected at the time. Some think the government was using some sort of substance to control the weather. While there's no way to say 'yea' or 'nay' to this theory, there are those who don't subscribe to it. Of course, the UFOlogists started mentioning alien activity.

Among those who don't believe the military were involved, the UFO theory seems to be the favorite. They opine that extraterrestrial activity was the cause of the blips over Kentucky, and quite possibly the other areas. It seems strange to them that the military would be conducting a nationwide training exercise that involved dropping so much chaff around the country. If they were, then were they preparing for an alien invasion? That's what some have theorized.

While we're not sure what the cause was, we were quite surprised when we heard the stories of the radar blips. The reason for that is because the day the interruptions were said to have happened, we had a very strange experience of our own.

We were out driving late at night, coming back from the town of Shepherdsville, when we spotted three lights atop Brooks Hill. As we stated before, we live near a major international airport, so aircraft lights aren't just common, they are constant. However, the behavior of these lights was rather odd. They were brighter than usual and aligned in a vertical formation overtop the hill. The road we were driving on, Conestoga Parkway, goes uphill at quite a distance before coming back down. We had reached the apex of the hill when we saw the lights. As we came down, we watched them methodically change formation, taking on the shape of a triangle.

Now, this was not a triangular craft. There are enough lights shining from surrounding businesses and neighborhoods, not to mention the towers atop Brooks Hill, to backlight the area. Though it was still quite dark, we could clearly see that there were three crafts, not one. We watched as they flew in the triangular formation for a while. They moved very quickly, and pulled very far ahead of us before we saw them break into a vertical line formation. We travelled down onto Preston Highway and lost them for a while behind the trees.

As we rode back into Hillview, we could see them intermittently through breaks in the wooded areas along the way. Through the years, industry has taken down much of the woods, but some of it remains. By the time we were into Hillview, we could see the three bright lights much farther ahead. One thing we thought was strange was the absence of any other crafts in the sky. Usually, there are a number of them flying in the night, but at this time, there were just the three we had seen atop the hill now pulling further away.

We decided to follow them. They were heading in the direction of the airport, and we figured that if they were regular planes and not UFOs, they would probably land there. So we continued down Preston into Okolona. That's when things got even stranger.

The closer we got to Louisville International Airport, the closer we got to the crafts. Though they had pulled a ways ahead of us, we were now catching back up to them. Also, we had come under a very thick and questionable low-lying cloud cover. Kentucky weather is unpredictable, so we thought maybe this was just some rain coming in, or some sort of fog. In the distance, we watched one of the crafts vanish into this cloudiness.

We drove on until we caught up to one of the crafts. We rolled down the windows and heard a humming that was not like the sounds made by the airplanes that usually pass over Louisville. It was a heavy humming with an underlying metallic whistling. As we got closer, we got a better view of it. The plane, or whatever it was, appeared to be blocky, not like a normal airplane, with a vertical rectangular box on its end. There were no visible wings or fins. It looked like two black rectangular boxes placed together. The bright lights we had previously seen shone from the bottom and the front. We drew so close to it that we could glance out the driver's side window and see it clear as day. It was very low in the sky, maybe 1000 feet, possibly less. Our view of it was clear, and we rode along beneath it for close to a minute before it ascended into the misty clouds, taking its bright lights with it, and disappearing.

We drove around for a little longer to see if we could catch another glimpse of the crafts but they were gone. We drove to the outskirts of the airport, just south of Downtown, before turning back. We never saw them again, and it wasn't until we were almost back into Hillview that we even saw another aircraft. That alone was strange.

We discussed what it could have been on the way home. What we saw were not commercial airliners or UPS planes. The low, fog-like cloud cover was unusual enough, but the way it had come on suddenly, as if masking the crafts as well as the airport, made matters much weirder. That fog also began/ended about midway through Okolona, just past the airport. Something about this was very odd. The next day we saw a YouTube video about the mysterious radar blips and wondered if they were related to what we had experienced.

The mystery blips of 2018 remain without a convincing explanation. They crafts we witnessed very well could have been military planes, or they might not have been. Perhaps they were tied to the mystery blips.

BIG BONE FLYING SAUCER

A woman living on the border of Big Bone Lick State Park claimed that in 2018 she had been seeing UFOs regularly for two years, but had sightings even farther back than that. These UFOs appear as great lights shining in the sky. She is not the only one seeing these lights, either. Her husband, niece, nephew, and neighbor have all seen them as well.

The sightings began in the summer of 2016 when her neighbor's dog kept barking at something outside during the night. The dog seemed quite frantic, and whenever her neighbor looked outside, she saw nothing there. Unsure of what it could be, the neighbor reached the conclusion that the digs being conducted in the park next door were the cause of her dog's berserk behavior. However, she wanted to be sure that no one was trespassing on her property, so she set up trail cameras on her porch.

What the camera captured seemed relatively mundane. When the neighbor reviewed the photos, all she saw was a red circle of light in the upper right-hand corner of the frame. It looked like it could have been nothing more than someone shining a flashlight at her house, which would have been cause for concern, but it wasn't anything to be particularly upset about. However, when she showed the images to the woman who had UFO experience, they reminded her of something that had happened to her long ago.

In 1974, the woman and the man she would later marry were parked on someone's property at night. As they sat in the darkness, a bright light shined into their car. At first, they thought the person who owned the land had caught them. But the light came from something far more frightening than anyone who lived on the property. When they looked into the sky, they saw what the woman called "the mother ship" passing by. She said it was as big as a football field. She and the man never spoke of the incident to anyone.

Over the next forty years, the woman never gave the 1974 incident anymore thought. But when her neighbor showed her the pictures, it all came back to her. She began to recall the incident. In the summer of 2017, the lights returned.

Mysterious lights began shining in the sky around her home. The lights would move about, flashing red and green like a strobe light. It was not her imagination, either. Both her husband and nephew observed them through binoculars. They watched as the lights floated over the treetops, pulsing red and green. Her niece had also witnessed the lights while working near the barn. She thought they were from a helicopter, and the rest of the family hoped that's what the lights were, as well. An incident at the end of January would change their minds, though.

As she was watching the sky, the woman thought she saw something fly by in the corner of her eye. She looked around and saw it again, in her peripherals, and thought it to be a saucer-shaped craft. She looked towards it, but it was gone. It soon appeared again in her periphery vision. She could never seem to be able to look straight at the object. But that changed about a week later when she saw it clearly in the sky. It was a silver saucer with three windows.

Since then, the family has kept watch on the sky around their home, awaiting the saucer's return. The pictures were inconclusive, though they do show lights and what looks to be objects in motion. In one, it does appear that there is a saucer in the sky, but still hard to tell. Allegedly, the family continued to see the lights for a time, perhaps it is still ongoing at the time that this is written. The niece believed the lights to be from a helicopter, but the others maintain they were not. These are lights like they haven't seen before. There may be no answers yet, but they are certain it is something extraterrestrial.

GOBLINS FROM THE UNDERGROUND

We already covered the Kelly Creatures in a previous chapter, but it does not seem that the significance of that 1955 encounter ends with the Sutton and Taylor families, the farmhouse, or even with the towns of Kelly and Hopkinsville. As we dug for more alien evidence and reports in the Bluegrass State, we came across some information that not only leads back to that case, but also opens a door to a labyrinth of alien visitations, cover-ups, and cloak-and-dagger operations. Since this goes much deeper than the Hopkinsville Goblins, we decided to keep this report separate.

Obviously, we are not the type to shy away from crazy stories, wild tales, or sensational urban legends. We deal in the paranormal, including cryptozoology, parapsychology, and the extraterrestrial, so one has to be willing to report even some of the most outlandish accounts to remain well-rounded in the field. That's not to say that we believe this detailed report to be far-fetched, it just points to a very complex theory regarding alien interference on our planet. However, this story supports one of our own theories regarding alien life on Earth, and we will get into that later. Because of this, we knew we had to include this report upon finding it. We searched for more online information and found that the portion regarding the "new goblins" came from only one source: a man named Greg Newkirk.

Dana Matthews and Greg Newkirk are paranormal investigators who own the Travelling Museum of the Paranormal and Occult, and they made a documentary on this case, called *Hellier*. It was at their site, *Week in Weird,* that this information was found, and, we reiterate, this site is the only location where we found any information on the new goblins in Hellier. So, we will begin by saying that we do not claim to support or challenge this story. We are only reporting what has been claimed, and in doing so we want to ensure the readers know that Greg Newkirk reported this story, and no one else, that way proper credit is given.

So as not to completely tell the story Matthews and Newkirk worked so hard to investigate, we will only give you the basic details and then encourage you to check out their writings and documentary on this case. It began in 2012 with an email sent to Newkirk from a man they called David, who said his home in Pike County, outside the town of Hellier, had been terrorized by small creatures that looked like hairless children; these beings had no facial features other than lipless mouths and large black eyes. The creatures were coming to the children's bedroom windows and chirping back and forth to one another, scaring the children. They were also leaving strange tracks in the snow and trying to gain entry into the house. They even broke into the family's shed out back and stole many items, and eventually took their dog as well.

Police were unwilling to help, and the encounters were becoming too much for the family. David then confided in a friend of his about the incidents, and the friend relayed the information to a man by the assumed name of Terry Wriste. Wriste once investigated cases involving extraterrestrials, but unfortunately had retired from such work. He then passed along Newkirk's information to David, and so he emailed Newkirk about the situation.

These "hairless children" (as the daughter of the family called them) continued to come around the house and make mischief. They were dragging stones from the walkway across the yard, tearing at the screen door, and tapping on the children's windows. One night, around 1:30, David woke to the sound of their dog scratching at the back door, wanting to go out. David noticed his motion lights were on, so he looked out the window to see if he saw anyone. He spotted someone's shadow cast along the backyard, and heard the sound of someone going through a box on his porch. He hit the window in anger and then heard the screen door slam shut outside. A second shadow joined the first, and he heard the creatures chirping. As he watched the shadows move about the yard, he saw something else in his periphery.

Standing in the flowerbed just below the window was a pale humanoid figure about four feet tall and hairless. This was when David got a good look at its face and saw the black eyes and slit mouth. Too frightened to move, he watched the creature hop to the others, chirping all the way, before the entire group, five of them in all, retreated to the woods beyond his property. It was a couple days after this that his dog went missing, and when he searched for it, he found some of the family's stolen goods scattered around the entrance to an abandoned mine shaft close to his property. David then told Newkirk that he would allow full access to his home and the use of any recording equipment needed if he would investigate the incident, all he wanted was complete anonymity for the sake of his career and the reputation of his family.

It turns out that the only Terry Wriste that could be found was the pseudonym, Terry R. Wriste, who was an ex-military occultist interviewed for two books printed in the 90s: *Secret Cipher of the UFOnauts* and *The Secret Rituals of the Men in Black*, both by Allen H. Greenfield. Greenfield interviewed Wriste at the beginning of each book. In these interviews, the enigmatic Wriste admits his name isn't real, and claims that he was a part of a group of Vietnam vets formed in the early 70s whose initiative was to infiltrate and destroy underground alien bases around the world.

David also claimed to have photos, so naturally Newkirk wanted to see them. It took a while for David to respond because the attacks at the house had become so rampant that the family had to leave. However, he did return to retrieve his camera and saw some strange tracks on the ground and took pictures of them. The tracks appear to have been made by a three-toed foot about eight inches long and lacking the curvatures of a human foot. These tracks, as David said, led into the woods and past a stream behind his house. There was also another photo of one of the creatures supposedly climbing a tree, though it is very sketchy and hard to define.

This led Newkirk to dub this case the Return of the Kelly Goblins, stating that there were striking similarities between this and the 1955 Hopkinsville incident. The only issues with this comparison are that the appearance of these new goblins and the 1955 creatures are almost entirely different, save for the height. The Kelly Creatures resembled great horned owls, had shiny eyes, and flew and glided through the air. These creatures are hairless with dark eyes and hop instead of glide.

It is quite possible, however, that the Kelly Creatures were wearing helmets that gave them the appearance of having pointy ears and shiny eyes. If they had on helmets and suits, it would explain the metallic sounds of Lucky and Billy Ray's bullets ricocheting off their bodies.

There are a few points about this claim to consider. The first one that we noticed, though it seems rather small, is that when David first mentioned the dog, he had referred to it as 'her'. Later on, when he mentioned the dog was gone, he said "his disappearance". This could be a typo, or it could indicate that the story isn't true. But, state police in the area did confirm that they had answered a call about such a case, even if they weren't able to share details.

Another interesting point is that the footprints had dermal images, which Bigfoot hunters look for to indicate if they are genuine. So, the prints seem to be legitimate. But, the most inconvenient aspect of the case, and the most curious, is that no further correspondence came from David.

However, the search was not over, and the plot thickened. About a year after David's last email, the mysterious Terry Wriste contacted Newkirk. His email was very cryptic and weird, but it came with an attachment showing a piece of paper with some numbers writing on it. Wriste had encouraged Newkirk to look deeper, and he did. He noticed that the letter was similar in style to letters sent to John Keel, UFOlogist and author of *The Mothman Prophecies*, from a group known as the International Bankers. These letters had very peculiar structure, were poorly written, and most importantly, warned Keel to stay out of matters that "did not concern him".

The letter from Wriste told Newkirk to "use the numbers". At first, he didn't know what that meant. Then an associate of his suggested that the numbers could be GPS coordinates. When Newkirk punched the numbers into Google Maps, the map landed on Brown Mountain, North Carolina, a place rumored to be the location of an underground alien base.

In the days when only the Native settlers roamed the lands, they spoke of strange lights over Brown Mountain. They attributed this to the ascension of their ancestors' spirits. Even after the English settlers arrived, they saw the lights and determined they were phantom in nature. But after the UFO craze of the 20th century started heating up, these lights became associated with extraterrestrials. Soon, tales of abductions near the mountains began. People who frequent the mountain waiting for the aliens to come have reported lights hovering above them, and mysterious government men approaching them and asking strange questions about their experiences. But, these are not the most intriguing accounts reported from the mountain. That distinction belongs to Ralph Lael, who claimed that small alien creatures lived inside the mountain's caves.

Lael liked to explore Brown Mountain in search of rocks for his Brown Mountain Rock Shop. When scouring the caves, he would be gone for days, even weeks at a time. He claimed that he was able to communicate with the mountain lights telepathically and one night they led him through the forest, up the mountain, and into a crystal-filled cave where a race of aliens called the Pewam met him. The Pewam took Lael for a ride in their spaceship and advised him on how he could save the world. Lael wrote a book about his experiences in 1965.

But the wild tales of intergalactic visitors wasn't all he gained from his lengthy explorations. After one excursion, he emerged with an alien corpse. The body was about three feet tall, hairless, and had long, slender arms and legs. He kept the body preserved for many years under a glass case in the back room of his shop. A blurry black and white photo of the alien mummy exists, though it's hard to discern much from it, other than the head does have an odd, misshapen quality to it. After Lael died, his shop was bulldozed and the mummy disappeared.

Although Lael's claims seem like something out of an old sci-fi paperback, he was not the only person to speak of an alien base or extraterrestrial activity in and around Brown Mountain. For many years, locals have spoken of undercover operations taking place in the forests and black helicopters flying above the mountain. They believe these to be a result of the alien base inside the caves. A book written by someone calling themselves Commander X, published in 1990, lists Brown Mountain among the many locations of supposed underground alien bases.

What surprised Newkirk so much about these GPS coordinates was that he and Matthews had gone to Brown Mountain seeking out aliens five months prior to receiving Wriste's letter. According to their story, the enigmatic Wriste knew they had been there and was telling them they had been on the right path. Matthews and Newkirk received no more emails from Terry Wriste.

According to Newkirk, he got in touch with Allen Greenfield, who told him that the Terry Wriste who was writing him was probably not the same Terry Wriste he himself had previously interviewed. He said that Newkirk's Terry Wriste sounded more like a "man in black". He then recounted briefly his own visit to Brown Mountain, and to Ralph Lael, and spoke of a strange man that came to his motel room to discredit Lael, calling him a "local moonshiner". Greenfield felt that since the mysterious visitor had known his reason for visiting the area, was able to track him down, and sought to paint Lael in a negative light, that the man very well could have been a "man in black".

Next, Newkirk claimed he spoke with Geraldine Sutton-Stith, daughter of Lucky Sutton of the Kelly Creatures incident. During their discourse, she allegedly told Newkirk of a man who came to her house to tell her of his father's deathbed confession. According to this story, the man's father was part of a team from Fort Campbell sent to retrieve the wreckage of a UFO that crashed three miles from the Sutton farmhouse on the same night the families encountered the creatures. This team supposedly gathered up the debris and took it to Wright-Patterson Air Force Base.

It was during this conversation that the stories of the Black Mountain in Lynch, Kentucky came up. For years, locals have spoken of lights floating above the mountains, similar to that of Brown Mountain. They say that they even feel the mountain hum, and people will go up there and disappear. We too have heard a few tales about Black Mountain, sometimes called Lynch Mountain. People have spoken to us about buzzing sounds, strange sparkling lights hovering and dashing about the night sky, and even the feeling of electromagnetic energy pulsing around it. People have said they've thought the place haunted, because they hear strange sounds and voices up there, and they feel that electricity. But others believe it is an alien base. As for this case, the most interesting part about Black Mountain is that it is very close to Hellier, where the new goblins harassed David's family.

So what's the connection? It's quite simple, and we theorized about it a few years ago when we first heard about Black Mountain and the Kelly Creatures. If indeed the Hopkinsville Goblins were aliens, and the light Billy Ray saw that night was a UFO, then the creatures crashed, came upon the farmhouse and the incident began. The creatures then sought refuge in a nearby cavern. Mammoth Cave, which is about an-hour-and-a-half drive from Kelly, is probably connected to this cave somehow. Mammoth Cave is a part of the fabled Paranormal Highway, which consists of many UFO sightings and alleged alien bases. Theoretically, these Kelly Creatures could have dwelt underground, travelling the cave system, and found their way to Black Mountain and caused the lights, the humming, and the electricity.

Approaching this with an open mind, and considering for the sake of argument that this is all real, it is possible that all, or a very large percentage, of the alien activity reported in Kentucky since 1955 could be tied to the Kelly Creatures and the underground labyrinths of Mammoth Cave. Mammoth Cave is massive, hence the name, and there are four-hundred miles worth of cave system already known, with more caverns and passages being discovered on a regular basis. It is believed that only a small portion of the cave's entire compass has been charted.

Let's consider the appearance of the new goblins from 2012—David's goblins—they were pale, hairless, and with oily black eyes. Could such a drastic change in appearance stem from decades living underground? Or could they already be subterranean creatures and sought sanctuary in the caverns because it was their natural habitat? If this were the case, it would make sense that the creatures, being natural cave dwellers, would be able to navigate sections and passages in the caves we have been unable to yet.

Of course, this is just a theory, and it's one Newkirk scratches at in his article. What intrigued us about this article so much is that it lends credence to our Mammoth Cave theory. The presence of the new goblins is further evidence that there are possibly creatures living in the mines and caverns of Kentucky. If they are extraterrestrial, they probably began with the Kelly Creatures, if those creatures were not great horned owls. It could possibly even go all the way back to the Thomas Mantell case.

One other point we would like to consider is that numerous videos and reports have surfaced over the last several years regarding creatures of similar appearance to David's goblins found in abandoned mines, caves, and sewers. YouTube has a plethora of channels dedicate to the weird and creepy, many consisting of Top 5 and Top 10 videos of chilling paranormal and alien footage. Many include videos of creatures spotted in some underground location, and most are similar in description to these particular beings.

Again, we are not validating the claims of the new goblins case. David's and Wriste's letters could have simply been people perpetrating a hoax, but they could have been legitimate. Of course, the story of the Brown Mountain Lights, the Black Mountain Lights, and Ralph Lael's alien mummy have been around long before David or Terry Wriste sent any emails to Newkirk. But, if the stories told in those emails are true, there might be some alien civilization dwelling in the caves beneath Kentucky, and even further.

Of course, it could all just be wild tales.

ALI AND THE ALIENS

Though the events in this chapter didn't transpire in Kentucky, Muhammad Ali was a Louisville native and is buried in the city's picturesque Cave Hill Cemetery. The man many consider to be the greatest pugilist of all time was not only an expert with his punches, but he was also an avid believer in extraterrestrials, going so far to claim that he believed aliens were watching him.

Ali told UFO researcher, Timothy Green Buckley, about some of his experiences. Ali confessed to Buckley that he saw his first two UFOs fly over New York City just before dawn one morning in 1970. He was running through the park when he looked up and saw a bright light shining down from the sky. At first, he thought it was a helicopter, but could clearly see it was not. It was a craft like none he had ever seen. Seconds later, a second UFO passed by, this one with a red light glowing behind it as it flew. He brought this to the attention of his trainer, and they watched the large round objects emerge from behind the skyline and travel slowly across the sky for about fifteen minutes. Ali later found out that there had been several other UFO sightings that night, including several near LaGuardia Airport and one from a pilot at Newark Airport.

Ali then went on to add that all of his friends had experienced the sighting, and that it was no joke. He said the aliens were watching him, and told Buckley that you could see them in the early morning hours, "playing tag between the stars". Ali claimed that he had seen about sixteen UFOs up to that point. The closest encounter he had happened when he was riding in a car on the New Jersey Turnpike and a cigar-shaped UFO hovered above the vehicle. It was nighttime and the moon was full, and the craft cast a large shadow in the moonlight. Ali and those with him could see the shadow all around the car. Buckley later showed Ali video footage of alleged UFOs, and he was able to point out to the author the similarities with the ship in the footage and the objects he himself saw in the sky.

On back-to-back evenings, a cigar-shaped craft passed over Ali's training camp in Pennsylvania's Pocono Mountains. It had come down out of the sky in a brilliant flash of light and hovered just above the valley. It had no windows, but the champ believed there had to be people inside. The next night, the ship returned at the same hour. This time, Gene Kilroy, Ali's business manager, was there to witness the event.

Gilroy was used to Ali going on about alien visitors. Most of the time, Kilroy chalked it up to the boxer's vivid imagination. But on this night, he knew there was something unusual taking place in the skies above them. Once his client had pointed the UFO out to him, Kilroy saw it dancing around in the sky. He then changed his perception about Ali's claims.

Ali's fascination with UFOs was not a belief he was ashamed to admit. Not only did he confide in Buckley about them, but he also shared his feelings about it on national television. On September 7th, 1973, Ali was a guest on the *Johnny Carson Show*, initially to talk about his upcoming rematch with Ken Norton. The two men had boxed previously in March, and Norton had defeated Ali by split decision, also breaking Ali's jaw, and winning the world heavyweight title. After Carson introduced Ali, it was clear that Ali was not interested in discussing the bout. He was more concerned with his alien encounters.

Not long into the interview, Carson was asking Ali about the weigh-in, to which the challenger cut him off and began talking about UFOs. Below is a transcript of the conversation.

ALI: I've been studying UFOs. Did you know there are UFOs out here flying around? Unidentified objects.

CARSON: This would be the place for them, southern California.

ALI: No, no. I'm serious. They sighted a bunch over Georgia. I've seen 'em at night. They have real photos of them, and the government, and the people just completely seem like, don't talk about them. But, um, Mr. Harold Salkin of Washington D.C. is the head of the national UFO bureau and he brought me moving films. I actually have moving pictures of little saucers, of gray still objects coming into pictures that people took, and I'm just surprised that don't nobody talk more about them. Something they can...

CARSON: Another great insight into the fight game. Nah, I'm just kidding. No, I read that. But did you read the thing last night on the, on the news?

ALI: Nah, I...

CARSON: That some physicist said that what the people of Georgia might have seen were, there are...uh...uh...several thousand...satellite objects...

ALI: Naw...

CARSON: ...going around the United States, around the Earth, and sometimes they disintegrate and they come back into space...

ALI: Not fifty feet over the highway.

CARSON: Well they could. It's got to land somewhere.

ALI: No. They call it swamp gas and something they don't want...I don't know what it is, but, I think I do, but they actual...there are actual saucers and objects coming within our atmosphere and flying around and people got pictures, everybody sight the same thing in every city, the red and blue and green lights. But, the people, the authorities completely brush it off as if to say we are mentally off, but I know it's right because I've been seeing them.

CARSON: Well, why don't they land then, Muhammad? I mean, now if they're intelligent people, why wouldn't they land and step out and say, "Hi there"? Or, "Gah-men ding" or whatever they say? You know? Why wouldn't they make contact?

ALI: Ah, they probably figure they can't no sense out of the people here on this Earth.

CARSON: We've never talked about that on this show. I didn't know you be…you really believe in UFOs?

ALI: I have actual photos. I have moving films.

CARSON: Yeah but, can't, they can, you know, motion pictures. Come on, you're smart enough to know…

ALI: This isn't no trick. This is…

CARSON: …that in still pictures…

ALI: Not these.

CARSON: …they can phony those up.

ALI: These are not, these are not phony.

CARSON: <points at Norton> Ken, how do you feel about it? Do you believe there are flying saucers?

KEN NORTON: I'm an innocent bystander.

CARSON: (to Ali) But you've seen them?

ALI: Yep. And the night, the one you can see on Tuesdays and Thursdays is like a big bright star if you go out.

CARSON: Tuesdays and Thursdays?

ALI: It's like a big bright star. I'm serious.

CARSON: Are you sure you're up for this fight?

ALI: I'm…I'm serious.

CARSON: <pointing towards Norton> If you're thinking about that when your, Monday night comes, he's gonna knock your head off.

ALI: No, I'm serious.

CARSON: You're gonna say, (looks up), it's ten o'clock...and he's gonna give you such a shot.

ALI: No. No it's not, it's not ten o'clock, it's four and five in the morning when they come up.

CARSON: Four and five in the morning? Ah.

ALI: Seriously. It's like a big bright star, and you see it moving, and it will go up and disappear and get real small like a pinhead, and then it will come back and it will shake, and then it might go over here and it will go over here. Seriously! I'm serious. I'm not joking.

CARSON: Oh, I know you're serious in your belief. I..I...

ALI: This is not *my* belief...

CARSON: ...don't have a belief in it myself.

ALI: ...this is anybody who's got eyes' belief.

CARSON: Well, you can see a lot of things, but that doesn't always make them...objects from other planets.

ALI: Well, so, so, so much of that. What about the fight?

CARSON: Well, yeah, what about the fight?

That's where the YouTube video cuts off. We assume that was the end of the alien discussion.

Ali, ever the psychologist, was always looking for ways to psyche out his opponents. Perhaps this was one way to get into Ken Norton's head. Maybe Ali felt if he went on about something that the public perceives as silly, as they do UFOs, that maybe the fight would seem inconsequential to him, like Norton was nothing more than an afterthought. Seeing as how Norton had barely beaten him in their previous meeting, Ali might have wanted to step up the head games. However, if you watch the video, Ali seems sincere, and he appeared clearly agitated before bringing up the topic. It's possible he could have been legitimately expressing his belief in the subject.

Of course, the whole thing could have been set up. If you are someone who's watched many talk shows over the years, the guests always seem to have some outlandish tale to tell or topic to discuss. It is possible some of these stories are scripted. Granted, it is often said that real life is stranger than fiction, so while these tales seem fantastic, they could be very true. Maybe Carson heard of Ali's interest in UFOs, considering this was only three years after his first sighting, which he discussed publicly, and he wanted to have a little back and forth banter to spice up the interview.

While many of Ali's accounts carry definite signs of the average UFO sighting, the particular object he discusses in the interview may not be a UFO. He could be talking about Venus, which is brightest in the sky about three hours before sunrise. But the hours do not precisely match. What about the object's movement? The movements Ali described match other accounts of UFO sightings.

We cannot fathom a reason Ali, a world famous sports figure, would make something like this up. We also have a hard time believing that all of the sightings he had were misinterpreted, considering they were numerous and, as previously stated, were witnessed by others.

It was Ali's religious beliefs that helped him try to understand the UFOs. According to him, the Nation of Islam viewed aliens from a religious perspective, which is an interesting theory. Ali's first sightings occurred prior to his conversion, when he was still Cassius Clay. Perhaps the visits were a sign for him to seek his intended spiritual path. Maybe they just liked him. Maybe all the aerial acrobatics were their way to "float like a butterfly and sting like a bee".

BLUEGRASS BLITZ

In 1978, the *National Enquirer* reported several UFO sightings out of central Kentucky. Many reports were from credible sources, and some even had evidence to back them up. This rash of UFO sightings became known as the UFO Blitz in the Bluegrass Triangle. The Bluegrass Triangle covers portions of Estill, Fayette, and Madison Counties.

The first incident involved two firemen in Madison County. They had received a call about a grass fire somewhere in Richmond. When they went arrived on the scene, they discovered there was no fire. What people had thought was flames were actually the burning red lights glowing off a nearby UFO. One of the firefighters, Robert Murphy, said that the bright red object was shaped like a saucer. As they approached, the craft took off. The two men followed it across town for more than an hour before they lost sight of it.

Elmer Hardy, who was then pastor of the Bybee United Methodist Church, was with his wife (whose name we could not find, though we tried), on their way to Sunday night service, when they spotted a UFO heading straight for them. When it reached their location, it hovered over their car, riding above them. Hardy described the craft as being ten stories high and more than twenty across, with countless lights all over it.

Kentucky State Trooper Jim Whittaker saw a car-sized UFO hovering over a field in Irvine. The ship had pulsing red, white, blue, and green lights across it. Whittaker was an experienced Naval Aviator, having flown more than 1500 hours, and he declared that this object was no helicopter or airplane. The officer then chased the strange craft across Estill County for roughly two hours. During the pursuit, he made an observation he thought was quite strange. As the ship flew through the night sky, anytime another aircraft would approach it, the UFO's lights would dim, and once the other craft had passed, they would light back up.

Two firefighters, a state trooper, and a pastor are certainly credible witnesses. There was another witness named Terry Kirby, who was also in Irvine, that may not have had the background of the others, being just a sixteen-year-old kid, but he solidified his claim with evidence. Terry was chopping wood when he saw a glowing, oval-shaped craft that he said was as big as a house, coming down from the sky above. Once he realized what he was looking at, he dropped his ax and went into the house to retrieve his camera. When he came outside, the craft was hovering in the sky, so he took a picture of it. This picture appeared in the *National Enquirer* volume that covered the article.

Other sightings from Irvine were mentioned in the article, but these were the most detailed. Chief of Police Marcus Cole went on record in the tabloid stating that several of the town's citizens phoned in reports of this mystery craft. Guy Hatfield, publisher of the *Citizen Voice & Times,* vouched for the witnesses, saying they were all very solid people and had no reason to claim they saw such an object if they did not.

We have little doubt that these witnesses saw the objects they reported. Many people reported it, and it seems highly unlikely that they would band together to make such a story up. Given that the Bluegrass Triangle covers such a large area, it's quite possible these people didn't even know each other, although we cannot verify that. It is likely, however, that this craft they saw was not alien in nature, but military. Remember the previous chapter about the Bluegrass Army Depot? It is right in the middle of the Triangle, lying just southeast of Lexington and Richmond, and due west of Irvine. Another interesting aspect to consider is that while the Triangle is in the central part of the state, it's actually in the east-central area.

This is not the only UFO blitz to have occurred in Kentucky, either. Let's move just a tad to the north, closer to Ohio. In December of 1998, twenty years after the Triangle Blitz, there were four UFO reports spanning two days (the 13th and 14th). These reports came out of Dry Ridge, Fort Mitchell, and Florence in Kentucky, and then another in Batavia, Ohio.

The first report came from Batavia around 10:35pm on December 13th when someone called the *Sci Zone* on 700 WLW AM, hosted by Bill Boshears, and reported to have seen a blue object descending from the sky over the Eastgate Mall in Cincinnati. He wondered if it could have been a comet.

The next sighting eliminated the possibility of the object being a comet (that and no known comet had passed by Earth when these sightings transpired; Hale-Bopp had ceased being visible to the naked eye almost a year prior). A woman driving down Hopeful-Church Road in Florence around 11:15pm reported seeing a large triangular object with blue lights hovering overhead. The lights traced a vertical pattern, and she thought there might have been some white lights present. It was hard to tell due to the light pollution in the area, but she states that the blue lights were clearly visible. She also added that she lived very near to the Greater Cincinnati-Northern Kentucky International Airport in Erlanger, and she could easily recognize a commercial airliner, and this was certainly not one. She did admit that it could have been military, though she didn't understand why it would hover there. The craft eventually took off towards the airport, but not on a direct path to land on a runway. Later that day, she saw black helicopters near where she had seen the craft. Sources stated that this witness, who wished to remain anonymous, was a very reliable source.

That morning, there were unexplained power outages in Florence, as well as Erlanger and Elsmere. Cincinnati Gas & Electric could not offer any explanation regarding the cause, only that the lines were burning and arcing for some reason. There is no direct connection between these outages and the UFO sightings. However, they are quite curious considering.

On the morning of the 14th, about 6am, a teenager reported a rounded object with blue flames descending near homes in Dry Ridge. Anonymity of both the person and exact location were maintained in the public report, but the witness said it looked like the object was going down, as if to land near the homes, and disappeared behind the houses. Exact details of the craft were hard to report because it was foggy that morning. Again, this is not believed to have been a comet. The witness's mother reported that around 4pm that afternoon there was an unexplained explosion felt rumbling through the town. No one knew the source of this event. The aforementioned power outage had no known connection to this explosion, either.

On December 15th, a report came in to Tim Hagemeister, Director of NACOMM, about a sighting the previous evening in Ft. Mitchell. The witness stated that he was outside from 11:50pm to 1am and at some point during that timeframe, he was looking to the east and saw a small star-like object in the sky northeast of Cincinnati. He said the light resembled that of a flickering candle flame, dimming and relighting. When it was at its brightest, it was brighter than any star in the sky, and when it would dim, it would move. The object, as he described, would move up and down and side to side, as if it were shaking (remember Muhammad Ali's description of the object he saw in the early morning sky?). The witness insisted that he did not imagine the shaking, and could clearly see it was doing so. He told Hagemeister that the object was no plane or helicopter. After he went to bed, his mother continued to watch it. He is not aware of how it finally faded from view.

All investigations into the sightings and tremors yielded no answers. News stations were asked if they had any information about earthquakes occurring and none of them did. The Greater Cincinnati Airport Control Tower had no record of the sightings, and didn't seem interested in discussing them. No one at the Grant County Sheriff's office or Highway Patrol office had received any calls about the sightings, either.

Again, we have a case of UFO sightings near Ohio. Batavia, just east of Cincinnati, lies about an hour west of the Great Serpent Mound, which we have already discussed the significance of that location. However, in between Batavia and the Great Serpent Mound lies Mt. Orab, which has a few UFO sightings of its own. If you believe aliens are visiting our planet, it sure seems like they love to visit southern Ohio and eastern, east-central, and northeastern Kentucky. What is it about our area that draws them in? Is it just chance? If there truly is a passageway located in Ohio, is it just convenient that they come through and travel down to Kentucky? Are they visiting those that live in the underground cave systems? It's all definitely interesting to ponder. Of course, it might all have a perfectly rational explanation.

AFTERWORD: OUR THEORIES AND CONCLUSION

Thank you for joining us on our first literary foray into the world of aliens. It is a topic we have long been interested in, much like the paranormal. With the paranormal, you explore the unexplained that exists in our world, while with the extraterrestrial, you explore phenomena from other worlds – at least, that's the idea. What causes these "alien encounters" is undetermined. They could very well be from our own planet, nothing more than advanced technology hidden from the public by the government. Some have even suggested time travel is responsible for UFO sightings. Of course, there are those who believe alien activity has religious implications linked to it. We don't know. We just know we find it interesting.

If you enjoyed the book, then we have good news. This will not be our only space adventure. Much like with our paranormal books, we intend to embark upon a long journey of alien exploration. *Aliens over Kentucky* merely marks the beginning of a coming series from the Frightening Floyds on the subject. So if you had a good time with this read—which we of course hope you did—then be on the lookout for more in the future.

Now, we refrained from offering our theories to these cases in each chapter to maintain an objective point of view. However, alien stories are not the same as ghost stories. With ghost stories, most explanations will be the same, and given that it's a supernatural subject, many of the theories revolve around intangible evidence. Theories regarding extraterrestrials are different. Explanations are very tangible. Aliens cannot be chalked up to old houses settling, gusts of winds from a cracked window, pareidolia, electromagnetic fields, residual energy, or any of the numerous theories parapsychology offers. With aliens, it was either an extraterrestrial being or something that can be touched and seen: weather balloons, military planes, animals, or any other earthly explanations. So, here we will offer brief theories on some of the cases.

THE DOGFIGHT OVER GENERAL ELECTRIC

We don't believe this was a hoax. The people involved with this incident were credible. Also, the extra evidence tied to other encounters around other GE plants, and given that a couple of the witnesses stated that the strange crafts they saw were headed in the directions of GE plants, leads us to believe that there is some connection between GE and these crafts. We do very much believe that these officers encountered some sort of craft that shot at them, or at least appeared to shoot at them. Now, was it alien in nature? That we don't know. It could have been military, as all alleged UFOs could be. In terms of UFOs, we do realize that it is possible that every single UFO could be classified military technology. Of course, it could be alien craft, that possibility is not ruled out; and, if they are military crafts, they could have been made with alien technology. It is all speculation at that level. We've never met with an alien ourselves, so who knows. But why would military shoot at the officers?

SPRING-HEELED JACK

We believe this was probably an ordinary man with some very interesting contraptions. In the Jane Alsop case, we believe Thomas Millbank was the culprit. Most likely, the fire was from a candle. He probably figured out how to blow flames by spitting a flammable substance at an open flame and decided it would be a good idea to do this to unsuspecting women. As for the other sightings, they were probably just impersonators. The high jumping, we admit, is very hard to explain. However, what of the man who was seen floating into the city on what looked to be a gyroscope? It is possible the alleged high jumping was an illusion created by some device that allowed the man to ascend into the air. Or, perhaps he was just very good at climbing. He may have been very agile and was able to scale walls so quickly that it could have looked like he was jumping, especially if it happened in the dark. Have you ever seen videos of street jumpers? Maybe he had some device on his feet that increased his vertical. But that leaves the incident of the man being shot and living. Given the period, it is possible he had on some sort of protective armor to deflect bullets; firearms then were incredibly inferior to those we have now. It's not as if these shooters were firing Desert Eagles or .357 Magnums. But, it very well could have been a demon, alien, or something supernatural.

THE KELLY CREATURES

We really want to believe this one, and we can't say that we don't. At the end of the chapter, we will offer another theory we have regarding the aliens in Kentucky, in which this case plays a part. But, as for the Kelly Creatures, it really does sound like these were great horned owls seen shortly after some sort of celestial body shot through the sky. However, we do keep an open mind. We do believe that the folks at the Sutton house would have known a great horned owl when they saw one, since they are indigenous to the area. While these creatures will attack if threatened, we cannot imagine they would continue an assault for such a long period. It really is a tough call. This explanation might seem like cognitive dissonance, but we really are torn on this one. When you take into consideration other evidence that connects to this case, it really does leave a heavy fog over top of it.

THE MEAT SHOWER

The incident in Kentucky was probably perpetrated by turkey vultures. It makes sense. However, that does not explain all the other meat and blood showers around the world. Turkey vultures are not indigenous to all areas. Tie these incidents into the cattle mutilations and then you have a theory, which we already discussed. Were the meat showers discarded livestock remains tossed away after alien visitors were done with them? Maybe, or perhaps not.

COAL TRAIN BATTLES THE SPACE CRAFT

We hate to be the party poopers on this one, but we think the train hit a UAV. The entire hubbub was probably because this incident was sensitive to the government. UAVs fit the description of the craft that was hit. Of course, it might have been an alien ship. There is no evidence to validate or debunk that claim. It sure would be neat to think the train really hit an alien ship.

THE BLUEGRASS ARMY DEPOT

Honestly, we really believe this is nothing more than a military installation. We doubt there are any aliens held there. While it's certainly possible and not out of the question, we just don't think that's going on there. However, we do realize we could be wrong. Strong arguments for alien activity have been made.

ALL CRAFTS: CUBES, TRIANGLES, CYLINDERS, AND SAUCERS
In terms of all the various crafts spotted over the decades, we believe there is a mixed bag here. We don't know how to explain the cubes. We admit those are quite strange. The triangles we believe are military planes, particularly the TR-3B, but there are others shaped like triangles. Some ask why they would hover over people and scare them. We're not necessarily saying they are all American military planes. They could be from other countries and who knows what's going on with foreign affairs. Cylinders are probably blimps of some sort, or jets, but could very well be alien. Saucers, we believe, are the most likely to be alien. Granted, some could be balloons, but if there are any spaceships entering Earth's atmosphere, the saucers and cubes are the most likely. Of course, any of them could be alien and any of them could be military. This is an endless debate.

MT. STERLING, SAND MOUNTAIN LIGHTS, AND THE WHITE CREATURE
For this one, we think you have a combination of mistaken aircraft, natural phenomenon, and urban legend. The Mt. Sterling UFO could have easily been a normal aircraft mistaken for a UFO. The Sand Mountain Lights are probably a natural occurrence, a reflection of starlight, or fireflies. The white creature seen walking the dark roads of Sand Mountain is probably a large animal whose description has grown more frightening over time. We don't believe there's any connection between the three, but we could be incorrect.

THE STANFORD ABDUCTION
If there is a solid case to be made for the existence of extraterrestrials, and proof that they visit our planet, then this case is the one. We do not believe these women were lying; we don't believe they were imagining anything; we think their story is real. All the evidence supports their report. We

believe someone or something abducted these women. There are too many witnesses, these women showed the physical and mental effects, and their stories matched even under hypnosis. With this one, we truly believe.

THOMAS MANTELL
We feel about this one much the same as we do about the Stanford Abduction. Thomas Mantell did not die chasing a weather balloon. He died chasing something that the government wanted to keep under wraps. What reason would there be to classify a weather balloon? It's not like it's some advantageous technology that could help protect our nation in the case of a threat. Unless they were up there trying to figure out how to control the weather, there's no reason to be secretive about a weather balloon. No, this was a UFO. Whether or not it was alien, we can't say. However, we don't really believe this was a military craft. We're leaning towards alien on this one.

CATTLE MUTILATIONS
We find it hard to believe there is a secret organization going around committing these atrocities because they want to monitor the food chain for Mad Cow Disease. That just sounds ridiculous. Besides, they would have to be one well-funded and sophisticated group of expert mutilators to pull off these eviscerations. We don't believe it's any sort of apex predator, either. These killings are committed with some intricate devices and expertise precision. The sloppier cases are probably animals and maybe humans, but the incidents where the cuts are perfectly made, organs cleanly removed, and no traces of blood left behind are most likely not human or animal. Think back to the meat showers.

EASTERN KENTUCKY, THE UFO BLITZES, AND THE NEW GOBLINS
We will cover these in the closing theory.

MYSTERY BLIPS
We don't believe this was a result of chaff dropped from mysterious planes on a secret west coast training expedition. We're not saying chaff wasn't released, but if it was, there was a purpose for it. It was not random. We

mentioned what we saw that night, and that could have been entirely innocent, but it sure was odd. This case sounds like a cover-up, but that doesn't mean it involves aliens and UFOs.

ALI AND THE ALIENS
We don't think Muhammad Ali made any of this up. His description of the small light moving side-to-side, up and down, and shaking is the same as another person's description from the Northern Kentucky UFO Blitz of 1998. Also, he had witnesses to many of his sightings. Ali was an intelligent and articulate man. We think he did see something strange. He certainly didn't need the attention and he wasn't seeking fame. He was one of the most famous athletes in history and at the time one of the most famous people in the world. He had no reason to create tall tales. Maybe what he saw wasn't aliens, but it wasn't normal, either.

OUR CLOSING THEORY
So, let's suspend all disbelief for this one. Yes, we know all the explanations and that it is quite possible no aliens have ever visited Earth, or are even out there at all. Skeptics will maintain that there is no proof, and they are correct. No evidence has ever been ironclad, and so many video hoaxes have been created that the credibility of more convincing exhibits has been damaged by a lot of this ridiculous footage, particularly those of supposed aliens actually recorded walking through homes or appearing at windows.

Going off the research we did and making connections, this is an interesting theory we have devised. The Great Serpent Mound in Ohio is at the center of some alien portal, or hotspot. They either enter Earth through there (or used to) or they are drawn to it. Something about Kentucky attracts them. Perhaps it is the rural landscape, with all the hills and forests. Particularly though, we believe it is Mammoth Cave and the intricate, vast cave systems under the state. As stated before, we believe these creatures to possibly be of a subterranean nature (if they exist), or from a planet with subterranean conditions. This is what has drawn them to our state. They are also very active in West Virginia, where mountains and caves are aplenty, as they are in eastern Kentucky.

We entertained the idea of the Kelly Creatures finding themselves a little further from their bases than they wanted. But perhaps they really were great horned owls. If they were not, and they were aliens in suits, then it is possible they attacked the Sutton-Taylor family out of fear and then fled to a cave and lived there ever since. Maybe they found the cave system and that brought more of their kind here, and they now dwell beneath the earth. That is why so many strange sightings have been reported in Kentucky. Maybe the reported crafts are more ships arriving, or maybe other aliens searching for the race that lives underground. Perhaps some really are military monitoring the skies.

It's fun to entertain such notions. It all sounds like great science fiction, but what if it was true? As we said, we're suspending disbelief. How far-fetched is it to someone who believes aliens might exist? Think of the blitzes and eastern Kentucky's sightings. Why is it that most sightings fall into regions on the eastern side of the state, and so many are near to Ohio where the Great Serpent Mound is? There are many connections.

It's an interesting idea, but could very well just be completely crackpot.

Anyway, if you enjoyed the book, or even if you didn't, we'd appreciate a review on Amazon, Goodreads, or any other site you can leave your thoughts. It doesn't have to be an extensive review, just a few words. Receiving feedback really does help authors, not only because it helps their work become more visible but also because it lets us know what we're doing well and where there are opportunities for improvement. So even if you didn't like it, please still leave us a review.

Thank you for reading. If you know any other alien enthusiasts, then tell a friend.

ABOUT THE AUTHORS

Jacob and Jenny Floyd, known as the Frightening Floyds, are enthusiasts of all things strange and unusual – ghosts, monsters, and of course, aliens. They have written several books on the paranormal and plan to write more regarding extraterrestrials. They live in Louisville with their three dogs (Tarzan, Pegasus, and Snow White—aka BooBoo) and four cats (Baloo, Narnia, Pandy, and Maleficent). You can follow them on Facebook at their Frightening Floyds page.

BIBLIOGRAPHY

After researching reports of aliens and UFOs in Kentucky, we were surprised by the amount of material out there. While there seems to be so many sources regarding the paranormal, there is at least twice as much information on aliens. As always, we checked a number of sites and cross-referenced their reports with others for accuracy. Any misinformation is unintentional, and we have reported the cases in line with the information contained in the sources listed below. We do not attempt to validate these claims or the sources, nor do we seek to discredit them. This book is for entertainment and is not intended to be a historic or scientific reference, nor an encyclopedic collection of information.

"Little Green Men in the Blue Grass: A History of UFO Sightings in Kentucky" by John Lasker at leoweekly.com

"Springheeled Jack" at unusualkentucky.com

"Police Helicopter Encounters UFO" at overflite.com

"Jefferson County, KY Helicopter/UFO Dogfight" at phantomsandmonsters.com

"UFO Puts on Show – Jefferson Police Officers Describe Close Encounter" by Gardiner Harris, published in *Louisville Courier-Journal*, published March 4th, 1993

National Investigation Committee on Aerial Phenomenon

"1973 UFO – The Schenectady Flying Saucer" by Cheryl Costa at syracusenewtimes.com

"Lynn, Massachusetts, June 15ᵗʰ, 1964 – Saucer Hovers above Pavement" at ufocasebook.com

Ken Pfeifer of *World UFO Photos and News*

UFOevidence.org

"The Legend of Spring-Heeled Jack, the Victorian Demon Who Terrorized London" by Aimee Lamoureux at allthatsinteresting.com

"Spring-Heeled Jack" at foilhatninja.com

"Spring Heeled Jack" at science.howstuffworks.com

"The Attack of Spring Heeled Jack" by Brian Dunning at skeptoid.com

"Spring Heeled Jack" by Jason Bellows at damninteresting.com

The Mystery of Spring-Heeled Jack: From Victorian Legend to Steampunk Hero by John Matthews, published by Destiny Books

"Spring Heeled Jack: The Devil? A Clever Hoax? Or a Lone Alien in 19ᵗʰ Century England?" at metimeforthemind.com

Sharon McGovern ("The Legend of Spring Heeled Jack") claims that a letter to the editor of the *Sheffield Times* in 1808 talks of a ghost by that name years previously; McGovern neither specifies the day in 1808 so that the letter can be verified nor lists any secondary source (for this or anything else). In addition, the *Sheffield Times* did not launch until April 1846.

Jacob Middleton, "An Aristocratic Spectre", *History Today* (February 2011)

David Cordingly, "Lives and Times: Spring-Heeled Jack", *The Scotsman* 7 October 2006. Excerpted from the *Oxford Dictionary of National Biography*

Rupert Mann, "Spring Heeled Jack", *Oxford Dictionary of National Biography* (Oxford: Oxford University Press, 2004; ISBN 0-19-861411-X)

Burke, Edmund; Ivison Stevenson (1839). *The Annual Register of World Events: A Review of the Year*. London: Longmans, Green. p. 23; pp. 26–27

The Morning Post of 7 March 1838, in Mike Dash, 'Spring-heeled Jack', *Fortean Studies* 3, p.pp.62–3

"1961, June: The Spring-Heeled Spaceman" at anomalyinfo.com

"The Sutton (Kelly/Hopkinsville) Encounter" at nicap.org

Nickell, Joe (November – December 2006). "Siege of 'Little Green Men': The 1955 Kelly, Kentucky, Incident". *Skeptical Inquirer.* Committee for Skeptical Inquiry

Offut, Jason (2019). *Chasing American Monsters*. Minnesota: Llewellyn Publications. pp. 113–114. ISBN 978-0-7387-5995-1

Dunning, Brian. "Skeptoid #331: The Kelly-Hopkinsville Encounter". *Skeptoid.* Retrieved June 26, 2013

Schmaltz, Rodney; Lilienfeld, Scott O. (April 17, 2014). "Hauntings, homeopathy, and the Hopkinsville Goblins: using pseudoscience to teach scientific thinking". *Frontiers in Psychology.* 5. doi:10.3389/fpsyg.2014.00336. PMC 4028994. PMID 24860520

"Story of Space-ship, 12 Little Men Probed Today". *Kentucky New Era.* August 22, 1955. Retrieved March 31, 2010

Hendry, Allan (1980). Ronald Story (ed.). *The Encyclopedia of UFOs*. Garden City: Doubleday & Company, Inc. pp. 190–92. ISBN 0-385-13677-3. Archived from the original on September 27, 2007

Lagrange, Pierre (2005), « Les petits hommes verts débarquent ! » (Little Green Men Have Landed!), *L'Histoire* n° 304, décembre 2005, pp. 26–27; Lagrange, Pierre (2016), « Qui croit aux petits hommes verts? De l'iconoclasme sociologique aux cultures visuelles. » (Who Does Believe in Little Green Men? From Sociological Iconoclasm to Visual Cultures), in Gil Bartholeyns (dir), *Politiques visuelles*, Paris, Presses du Réel, 2016, pp. 229–271

"The Eerie Story Behind the Small Town Everyone is Flocking to for the Eclipse This Summer" by Maria Carter at countryliving.com

"The Kelly-Hopkinsville Encounter: A Historical Perspective" at thehistorybandits.com
http://www.newcitystage.com/2015/08/23/review-it-came-from-kentuckythe-annoyance-theatre/

Valerii I. Sanarov, "On the Nature and Origin of Flying Saucers and Little Green Men," *Current Anthropology*, Vol. 22, No. 2 (Apr. 1981), pp. 163-167

https://www.reddit.com/r/creepy/comments/3yiibj/til_of_the_kelly_hopkins ville_alien_encounter_in/

"Turkey Vulture". *Washington Nature Mapping Program.* Retrieved 13 October 2014

Fort, Charles (1919). *The Book of the Damned.* New York: Boni and Liveright. pp. 45–46. OCLC 2062036; Fort, pp. 288–89

"Flesh Descending In a Shower; an Astounding Phenomenon in Kentucky--Fresh Meat Like Mutton or Venison Falling From a Clear Sky" (PDF). *The New York Times.* March 10, 1876

(21 March 1876). The Carnal Rain - Careful Investigation of the Kentucky Marvel by a Correspondent, *New York Herald*, p. 4, col. 1

Crew, Bec (December 1, 2014). "Blog: The Great Kentucky Meat Shower mystery unwound by projectile vulture vomit". *Scientific American*

Wilkins, Alasdair (March 21, 2012). "When It Rains Animals: The Science of True Weather Weirdness". *io9*

Mr. X (3 May 2015). "Debunked: The Kentucky Meat Storm of 1876". *Journal of the Bizarre*

zatzbatz (May 9, 2003). "Kentucky Meat Shower". Everything2.com

Weird History (2018-05-23). *Kentucky Meat Shower - The Day It Rained Mystery Meat*. Retrieved 2018-10-25 – via YouTube

Dunning, Brian (December 11, 2018). "Skeptoid #653: The Great Kentucky Meat Shower". Skeptoid

"The Mystery of the Kentucky 'Meat Shower'" by Kaleigh Rogers at vice.com

"Rain of Meat" at soul-guidance.com

"Read about the Mysterious Rain of Meat that Fell on the Village of Picún Leufú" at LosAndes Society, September 16, 2016

"Fortean" Fall of Flesh and Blood" from *Flying Saucer Review* (Great Britain), 1968 volume 14 no.6

The American Journal of Science and Arts, October 1841, page 404

"Extraordinary Phenomenon: Shower of Flesh and Blood" from *The Courier* (Hobart, Tasmania), 27 July 1850, Page 4 and *Vermont Watchman and State Journal* (Montpelier, Vermont), April 04, 1850, front page

"Chatham County "Blood Shower"" at nchistorytoday.wordpress.com

"Fall of Blood in Chatham County" by F.P. Venable from *Journal of the Elisha Mitchell Scientific Society* by Elisha Mitchell Scientific Society (Chapel Hill, N.C.), 1884, Volume 1, page 36

"A Fall of Flesh in California" from *The Glasgow Herald* (Ireland), Nov 17, 1869, page 6

The Cornwall Chronicle (Launceston, Tasmania), 25 October 1851, Page 679

Hobarton Guardian, or, *True Friend of Tasmania* (Hobart, Tasmania), 29 October 1851, page 3

The Petroleum Centre Daily Record (Petroleum Centre, Pennsylvania), March 29, 1869, Page 2

The Wheeling Daily Intelligencer (Wheeling, West Virginia), March 24, 1869, page 2

Clark, Jerome (1993), *Unexplained! 347 Strange Sightings, Incredible Occurrences, and Puzzling Physical Phenomena*, Detroit: Visible Ink Press, ISBN 0-8103-9436-7
Reece, Gregory L (August 21, 2007). *UFO Religion: Inside Flying Saucer Cults and Culture. I. B. Tauris.* ISBN 1-84511-451-5., 213 pp

"THE MYSTERY AIRSHIP LOG - 1871 through 1895" angelfire.com

"Railroader's UFO Collision: CSX?" at cs.trains.com

"Eastern Railroad Discussion: Train hits UFO, Paintsville, KY 2001" at trainorders.com

"Further Analysis of Train/UFO Collision Case" by Robby Vaughan at theufochronicles.com

"Was the 2002 Kentucky UFO Train Collision Genuine or a Hoax?" by Marcus Lowth at ufoinsight.com

"Cypher UAV" at dreamlandresort.com

"The Blue Grass Army Depot" at unusualkentucky.com

"Blue Grass Army Depot, Kentucky". *Program Executive Office, Assembled Chemical Weapons Alternatives*. Archived from the original on September 10, 2008. Retrieved October 30, 2013

"Blue Grass Army Depot". *The Center for Land Use Interpretation*. Archived from the original on February 11, 2012. Retrieved October 30, 2013

"BGAD History". *bluegrass.army.mil*. Archived from the original on May 13, 2013. Retrieved July 12, 2013

"Blue Grass Army Depot Vital to Madison County Culture and Community" at bricksandmortarpreservation.wordpress.com

Weird Kentucky: Your Travel Guide to Kentucky's Local Legends and Best Kept Secrets by Jeffrey Scott Holland, published by Sterling (May 6th, 2008) ISBN: 978-1402754388

"Mt. Sterling, KY" at ufo-hunters.com

"The Sand Mountain Ghost Lights" at theblacktriangle.blogspot.com

"The 1976 Stanford, Kentucky Abductions" at theblackvault.com and at ufocasebook.com
"Mantell Pt 3". Archived from the original on 2005-01-12

Ridge, Francis (2010). *The Mantell Incident* (PDF) (1st ed.). NICAP. p. 1. Retrieved 3 August 2018

"News Release of Clinton County Army Air Field dated 8 January 1948".

"Report of Albert Pickering".

Global Security. "Project Skyhook". *Intelligence.* GlobalSecurity.org. Retrieved 2013-09-07
"Kentucky: National Guard History eMuseum. Captain Thomas Francis Mantell Jr".

Commonwealth of Kentucky. Archived from the original on 2011-07-21. Retrieved 2011-06-03. On Saturday, 29 September 2001, the Simpson County Historical Society unveiled a historical marker in honor of Thomas F. Mantell, Jr.

Kevin Randle. "An Analysis of the Thomas Mantell UFO Case" (PDF). National Investigations Committee on Aerial Phenomena. Retrieved 2011-01-08

Berry Craig (9 November 2011). *Hidden History of Western Kentucky.* The History Press. pp. 40–43. ISBN 978-1-60949-397-4. Retrieved 2012-06-03. The blue and gold plaque stands outside the Simpson County tourist office.

Nicap.dabsol.co.uk/mantell1.htm

Nicap.dabsol.co.uk/mantell4.htm

"Captain Thomas Mantell's Last Words" *C.R.I.F.O. Newsletter* 1.9 (December 3, 1954)

Crain, T. Scott, Jr. "A Mantell Diary", *MUFON UFO Journal* 217 (May 1986): 9-13,17

Gillmor, Daniel S., ed. *Scientific Study of Unidentified Flying Objects.* New York: Bantam Books, 1969

Gross, Loren E. *UFOs: A History – Volume 1: July 1947-December 1948.* Scotia, NY; Arcturus Book Service, 1982

Jones, William E. "Historical Notes: Thomas Mantell" *MUFON UFO Journal* 264 (April 1990): 18-19

Keyhoe, Donald. *The Flying Saucers are Real.* New York; Fawcett Publications. 1950a

Keyhoe, Donald. *The Flying Saucers are Real.* True (January 1950b); 11-13, 83-87

"These 11 Unexplained Natural Phenomena in Kentucky Will Baffle You" by Jenn Shockley at onlyinyourstate.com

"Crop Circles" at sos-paranormalinvestigations.weebly.com

"Reported Crop Circles for the State of Kentucky - Hill Top / Flemingsburg, Fleming County (May, 2003)" at iccra.org

"Ohio Crop Formation at Legendary Serpent Mound" at Kenny.anomalyresponse.org

"Crop Circle in Flemingsburg, KY" by Kenny Young at Kenny.anomalyresponse.org

"Locust Grove, Adams County, Ohio – August 23rd, 2003 at iccra.org

"Sacred Serpent Mound Linked to Legends of Giants and Aliens" by Katalina Aster at articles.spiritsciencecentral.com

https://www.legendsofamerica.com/oh-serpentmound

"*The Mystery of the Serpent Mound: In Search of the Alphabet of the Gods*" by Ross Hamilton https://www.history.com/topics/serpent-mound

"*Giants On Record*" by Jim Viera

https://grahamhancock.com/vieiranewman1

https://www.newspapers.com/clip/24494275/1974_cattle_mutilation_article_general/

"Texas UFO Museum & Research Library – Animal Mutilations" at roswellbooks.com

"F.B.I.: The Vault – Animal Mutilations" at vault.fbi.gov

"Cattle Mutilation Theories Exposed on the *Unexplained Files* Airing Sept. 4th on Science Channel" by David Moye at huffpost.com

"Death on the Great Sand Dunes: the Strange Case of Snippy the Horse, the First Cattle Mutilation" by Greg Newkirk at weekinweird.com

"Livestock Killings Puzzle All" by Bryon Crawford, published in the *Cincinnati Enquirer – Kentucky Edition* on July 10th, 2001; can be found at unusualkentucky.tripod.com

"Australian Witness Photographs Cylinder UFO" at mufon.com

"Cylinder UFO Videotaped over Small New York Town" at mufon.com

Nuforc.org

"Caught in the Headlights? Experts Explain Deer-Cam UFO" at nbcnews.com

"Cylindrical UFO Videotaped By Kentucky Amateur Astronomer Allen Epling (VIDEO)" by Lee Spiegel at huffpost.com

"Unidentified Aerial Phenomena in the UK Air Defense Region: Executive Summary"(PDF). Retrieved 2011-09-13

"UAP In the UK Air Defence Region: Executive Summary, Defence Intelligence Staff (2000), p. 7". Mod.uk. 2007-02-20. Archived from the original on 2011-09-06. Retrieved 2011-09-13

"The Belgium UFO Wave". *www.ufoevidence.org*. ufoevidence.org. Archived from the original on 24 August 2014

"Sunday Express' article on Belgium UFO". *Sunday Express*. 17 September 1995. Retrieved 21 March 2008

"UFO Sightings: Dark Triangle UFO Seen in Kentucky" by Anna Dominguez at itechpost.com

"Dark Triangle UFO over Neighbourhood in Louisville, Kentucky Following Google Map Car, UFO Sighting News" by Scott Waring at ufosightningsdaily.com

"'Dark Triangle' UFO Loomed Menacingly In The Clouds Over House In Louisville, Kentucky — Mystery Craft Was Stalking Google Map Car, Blogger Claims" by John Thomas Didymus at inquisitor.com

Google Maps

Black Triangle Kentucky 2-22-07 Sighting uploaded by Tom Levine at youtube.com

"Hovering Triangle UFO Moves Away 'Instantaneously'" by Roger Marsh at openminds.tv

"Triangle UFO in Ewing, Kentucky" at noufors.com

"Triangle UFOs over Kentucky" at unusualkentucky.blogspot.com

"Witness Sights Two Triangle UFO near Chaplin, Kentucky" at ufocasebook.com

"UFO Sightings Abundant in Eastern Kentucky; MUFON Investigating" by Tim Preston at dailyindependent.com

"UFO over Greenup, Kentucky – March 23rd, 2018" at theblackvault.com

"UFOs over Kentucky Valentine's Day Weekend 2011 – Social Paranormal Network Report" by Theresa J. Thurmond Morris at ufodigest.com

"Kentucky Witness Says Glowing Object Landed" at mufon.com

Ufo-hunters.com

"UFO Sighting and Possible Communication – Eastern Kentucky" at theblackvault.com

"Mysterious Blip Appears in Kentucky's Night Skies Spurring Theories" by Jon Webb of the *Evansville Courier & Press* at whas11.com

"A West Virginia Air Guard C-130H was Responsible for Massive Chaff Cloud over Midwest" by Joseph Trevithick and Tyler Rogoway at thedrive.com

"Remember Those Mysterious Radar Blips? Kentucky Wasn't Alone" by Jon Webb at courier-journal.com

"Northern Kentucky UFO Sightings?" by Jeremy D. Wells at journal-times.com

"Return of the Kentucky Goblins: New Leads in a Case of Strange Creatures, Crashed UFOs, and the Men in Black" by Greg Newkirk at weekinweird.com

Johnkeel.com

The Brown Mountain Lights by Ralph Lael

"Aliens, Ghosts, and Giant Fireflies: Solving the Mystery of the Brown Mountain Lights" at blueridgeoutdoors.com

"The Mystery Mummy: Did an "Alien" Body Turn Up Near a Famous UFO Hotspot" by Micah Hanks and mysteriousuniverse.org

Brownmountainlights.com

"'Aliens Watched Me': Boxing Legend Muhammad Ali 'Saw' Several UFOs Including Mothership" by Jon Austin at express.co.uk

Amazing Flying Saucer Experiences of Celebrities, Rock Stars and the Rich and Famous by Timothy Green Buckley

"Boxing Champion Muhammad Ali Had a Fascination with UFOs" by Micah Hanks at mysteriousuniverse.org

"Muhammad Ali on UFOs – September 7, 1973 – Budget Time Travel" uploaded by Hatala Testing on YouTube.com; footage taken from the *Johnny Carson Show.*

"UFO Blitz in the Bluegrass Triangle" at unusualkentucky.blogspot.com

"UFO Blitz Confounds Northern Kentucky Area" by Kenny Young at rense.com

"What Are Those Mysterious UFOs Doing Above Kentucky?" by Sara Marie Hogg, at calebandlindapirtle.com

"Exploring American Monsters: Kentucky" by Jason Offutt at mysteriousuniverse.org

"Mothman Sighting in Russell" at unusualkentucky.blogspot.com

PHOTO CREDITS

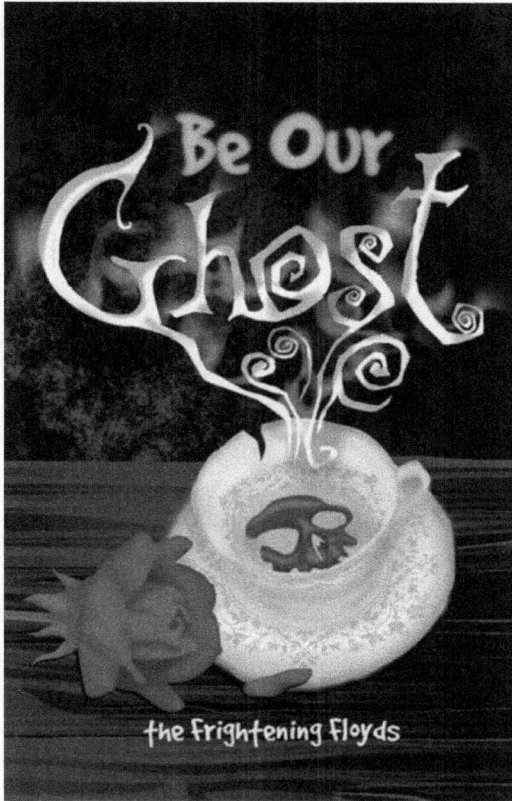

Be Our Ghost

the frightening floyds

The Frightening Floyds present *Paranormal Encounters*: a collection of 14 tales of true ghostly experiences. From a malevolent spirit remaining in an apartment, to a loving phone call from a lost relative; from a house with a sliding chair and slamming doors, to a snow globe moving across a bedroom; from a possible past-life experience to a ghostly stranger in a radio station, this anthology contains several strange and unusual stories that are sure to entertain fans of the paranormal.

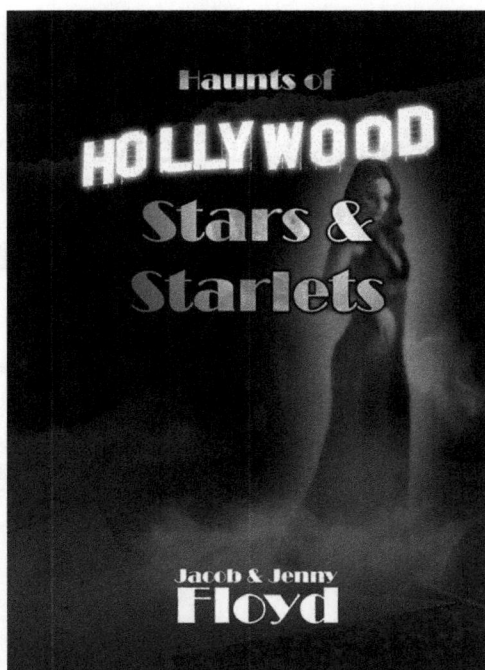

Haunts of

HOLLYWOOD
Stars &
Starlets

Jacob & Jenny
Floyd

Explore the dark side of Tinseltown in this collection of paranormal stories, conspiracy theories, curses, and legends about some of Hollywood's most iconic names: Marilyn Monroe, Rudolph Valentino, Charlie Chaplin, James Dean, Jean Harlow, Clark and Carole, Lucille Ball, Michael Jackson, Bela Lugosi, Lon Cheney, John Belushi, and the King himself—Elvis Presley—and many more. Join the Frightening Floyds as they take you on a terrifying journey through the city of glamour and glitz!

Thank you for reading! If you like the book, please leave a review on Amazon and Goodreads. Even if you don't like it, please still leave a review.

To keep up with more Anubis Press news, join the Anubis Press Dynasty on Facebook.